SURRENDER

What My Liver Transplant Taught Me about Control and Self-Acceptance

Jessica Zampieri

Copyright

Dedication

This book is dedicated to my donor, Dustin and his family.

In honor of your selfless gift, you will always be remembered.

Contents

Prologue

Cincinnati, Ohio

June 7, 2011

The periodic beeps and buzzes of a dozen different machines were like a steady metronome, marking the minutes as they crept by. As my thoughts came in and out of focus, I was filled with gratitude for each and every one of these seemingly mundane sounds emitted by the various machines that tracked my vital signs. Every mechanical chirp gave me definitive proof that I was still alive. Each soft whir reassured my disoriented brain that I was still in my room at the University of Cincinnati Medical Center, wearing a standard-issue, colorless gown beneath the unforgiving lights that shone overhead. The whispered encouragement of these machines let me know that my body hadn't given out on me.

Not just yet.

I clung to those tiny, concrete signals with all of my quickly fading might. They were the only thing that made any sense in this senseless situation. My sudden descent from perfect health into dire illness had been entirely unexpected, completely unheard of for someone my age. I was forced to concede that I couldn't take anything for granted where my health was concerned. Not anymore. Instead, I had to rely on the small but definitive sounds made by the equipment all around me, the results of an avalanche of tests, and the utterances of my diligent medical team to get a sense of just how close to death I really was, because by then, my own body and mind were refusing to give me straight answers.

There were countless things about this moment in my life that I never could have predicted. I couldn't have known that I'd be confronted with the possibility of my own death at the age of twenty-eight, or that all my years of striving for physical perfection would end up undermining my wellness to such a devastating degree. But one of the most surprising aspects of this crisis was the unexpected feeling of relief that washed over me as it all unfolded. After a lifetime of trying to be self-sufficient, at the top of my game, as close to perfect as possible, I finally had to admit that I couldn't control this situation on my own. Relinquishing control like this had always been one of my greatest fears. But when I was forced to accept help at long last, the relief I felt was nothing short of revelatory. I took such solace in the simple fact that I didn't have to go it alone anymore.

"Jessica?" I heard my mother's voice say, as if from a great distance. "Jessica, we have to get through this..."

With great effort, I swung my dizzy gaze to the side of my hospital bed, every tiny movement sending jolts of pain crackling along my nerves. My mother, Susan, was perched there beside me, just as she had been ever since the morning I called her from my GI's office to tell her the news that I desperately needed a liver transplant. From that very first moment, my mom had been at my side, doing everything in her power to see that I made it through this ordeal alive, that her firstborn daughter wouldn't be taken quite so soon.

But even my mom's unwavering determination couldn't stop my body's decline in its tracks. Despite her extensive knowledge and experience, the matter was simply out of her hands. A mother's love and guidance can conquer many things...but not this. Illness doesn't defer to anyone, even the most fiercely devoted mother. My liver was set on failing, and it seemed to share my determination and work ethic. I almost had to admire its stubborn sense of purpose, even if I wasn't *at all* on board with the goal it had in mind.

The arrivals and departures of my friends and family were all I had to mark the days I spent in the Intensive Care Unit. Nobody tells you how easy it is to lose your grip on something as concrete as time while you're in the hospital. Minutes and hours, days and nights, whole weeks start blending together the moment you're confined to a hospital bed.

And I wasn't just confined in the physical sense of the word; I was trapped in a state of weakness and confusion. All the concrete, anchoring facts I'd always taken for granted had left my mind. I couldn't have told you what year it was, what city I was in, or who was sitting in the White House.

The entire world felt like it had shrunk down to the size of my hospital room, where I'd been lying for days on end as my body did its best to keep going despite my liver's self-destructive instincts.

"I know this is hard to talk about," my mother continued, her assertive words cutting through the fog that clouded my mind, "But there are things we need to discuss—"

"It's OK," I murmured, closing my eyes tightly to stop the room from spinning all around me, "I'm OK."

I was lying through my teeth, of course. Restrained to a hospital bed, barely able to form complete sentences, I was a long way from being OK. But since arriving in the ICU, I'd been using every spare ounce of energy I had to convince the people around me that I was fine. That I was still in control. Still positive. Still completely sure that everything was going to be all right. The toxins swirling through my body had me feeling like I was knocking back a shot of tequila every minute, but that wasn't going to deter me. Even as my blood turned to poison in my veins, I wanted to contribute to the effort of saving my own life.

What can I say? I'm a team player.

Even as one of my vital organs continued its descent toward failure, I desperately needed the people around me to believe that I was going to pull through. By then, people all over the world were praying for my recovery. Family and friends, of course, but also people I had never met. I needed all the hope that carried those prayers over countries and continents to manifest in my ailing body. When I managed to quiet my disorderly thoughts and concentrate, I could actually *feel* those prayers at work, and I believed that they would deliver me through this. I also felt a responsibility to all the people praying for me. I had to do my part to pull myself back from the brink of death. I couldn't let all those people down. If I could just show my guests, my doctors, and my nurses that I was OK, maybe I could will that to become the truth. It was tortured logic, I know. But that's what massive liver failure will do to a girl.

Of course, the one person who could see right through my courageous act was sitting right beside me, urging me to get back to the task at hand.

"Let's talk about what you want for the service, then," my mom went on, glancing down at the notes she'd been diligently taking.

The "service" she spoke of was my memorial service. My mother and I were sitting in my hospital room, planning my own funeral. No one had prompted me to do this, but I'd insisted all the same. There was a dark feeling of dread hovering at the edges of my consciousness. In the same way that some people can sense when it's about to rain, I could feel death circling over me, waiting to descend. I didn't want to leave my family high and dry after I was gone. Getting my funeral plans down on paper was something concrete I could do to make their lives a little easier in what I knew would be a terrible time. They were doing so much for me as I fought for my life in the hospital—this was the least I could do in return.

The fact that getting these funeral arrangements down on paper wasn't alarmist or hyperbolic would have been hard to wrap my head around on the best of days. I was a twenty-eight-year-old woman, after all. At this point in my life, I should have been planning for a job promotion, a dream vacation, maybe even a wedding. But a funeral? Nobody my age could anticipate something like that. To be young is to be wholly convinced that you're invincible, even when presented with evidence to the contrary. And at that moment, I was up to my eyeballs, suffocating in evidence.

Still, I felt oddly calm as I related my last wishes to my mother. It just seemed like the practical thing to do, and I'm all about practicality. As I described my ideal funeral service, my sense of peace deepened. I may not have been able to heal my liver through willpower alone, but I certainly knew how to plan a party. I requested that every guest bring a photograph of us together to the service and share a favorite happy memory of me with my parents. In my casket, I wanted to be wearing trendy distressed jeans (the ones with all the perfectly placed rips and holes), a white T-shirt, and my favorite pair of pointe shoes. These may not have been the most conventional fashion choices, given the occasion, but at that moment they felt perfectly right.

"You know what today is, don't you honey?" my mom whispered as I drifted ever farther away from this plane of existence.

By then, it was almost impossible for me to respond. My voice was sandpapery and strained. Even forming the simplest of sentences was an effort of enormous concentration, one that left my brain pounding painfully against my skull. I felt as though I had slipped entirely out of time. I was only vaguely aware of my mother's hand resting on mine, the presence of my father, siblings, aunts, and grandmother who came and went from my hospital room. I couldn't even be sure if the people around me were really there or just hallucinations. Whether they were real or not, everyone around me seemed to be holding their breath, waiting for me to respond.

Mom's pen paused above her notepad as she waited for me to reply. It was the first pause I'd seen her take since this whole ordeal started. A longtime nurse and nursing instructor, Mom had taken on the role of my knowledgeable advocate. She'd been by my side day in and day out, keeping my doctors informed of my status, translating medical jargon for my friends and family, taking care of me just as she had my entire life. Looking over at her now, I saw that her face was set against the sadness and fear I knew must be weighing on her heart. This wasn't the first medical emergency she'd witnessed, far from it. But it *was* the first that one that involved her oldest daughter. Mom was used to maintaining a certain amount of professional distance from the patients she watched over. But those protective measures were impossible now that I was the patient in question.

"Today..." I breathed softly, struggling to keep my words from slurring together, as they'd taken to doing by that point. "Today is..."

"It's been four years," she went on, shooting a perfunctory glance at the wall of machines that monitored my every breath.

We stopped to give this fact its proper weight. To observe the unhappy anniversary even as we dealt with the crisis at hand. Three years ago to the day, my mom's father—Grandpa Charlie—had passed away. And today, I was lying in the ICU as my mother and I planned out my funeral should I not live to see tomorrow. To call this convergence a coincidence didn't feel quite right. I could feel much larger forces than mere chance calling the shots, by then. I knew, deep in my weary, burning bones, that there was a reason things were unfolding this way.

I'd always believed that God had a plan for me, but that trust had never really been put to the test before. Up until now, my life had unfolded in a clear, straightforward path. My faith had never been tested, but that also meant it hadn't had the chance to clarify. Now, I was finally realizing what strong stuff my faith was made of. I knew, even as my liver revealed itself to be more deeply damaged than I could have ever guessed, that this event was not an aberration from my path—it was part of it, just as every other moment in my life had been up until that point.

Some people might question God's plan for them, in a moment that seems so removed from the trajectory of their life. But lying there in my hospital bed, planning my own funeral on the anniversary of my grandfather's death, listening to the mechanical symphony of the medical equipment all around me, I didn't find myself questioning God at all. Instead, I felt called to do something I'd scarcely managed in my short twenty-eight years on this planet. Little by little, I began to loosen my grip on the situation. To accept that no performance of being OK and was going to save me from whatever was coming next. For perhaps the first time in my life, I accepted the fact that I was not in charge. Having spent my entire life needing to be in control of every moment, I didn't know what to expect when I finally let go.

But something told me I was about to find out.

"Jessica," my mother said again, a new sharpness in her voice as she leaned in toward me. "Jessica, can you hear me?"

I meant to answer, but the darkness creeping in around the corners of my vision fascinated me to the point of distraction. The reliable sights and sounds of my hospital room blurred together, and I let my body sink back against the hospital bed as the world began to dissolve around me.

For once, there was nothing I could do. Nothing I could fix or work to perfect. Nothing that could change the fact that my body was not longing for this world. Fighting back wasn't an option.

So instead, I chose to surrender.

***

Chapter One

The Turning Point

One week earlier...

I tossed my purse absentmindedly into the back seat of my car while my mind scrolled through the day's seemingly endless to-do list. Sinking heavily into the driver's seat and slamming the door shut, I forced a deep breath into my lungs, willing my nerves to get ahold of themselves, already. It was another busy workday, and I couldn't afford to let dread and doubt get the best of me. I had way too much to get done for all that, and I was already having a hard enough time focusing as it was. My mental state had been growing steadily less reliable of late, which was alarming to say the least. After a lifetime of being on the ball and always on top of things, confusion and disorientation were now muddying my mind. Swallowing a sigh, I pulled down the visor above my seat to consult the vanity mirror. While my appearance was as neat and professional as ever, I hadn't quite managed to banish the look of worry from my eyes...let alone the yellowish tint that had crept into them of late.

Yep, I thought to myself with a grim half-smile. *I look about as anxious as I feel.*

A cloud of unease had been hovering over me

throughout Memorial Day weekend. Even as I smiled and celebrated with my friends and family, I couldn't quite shake the feeling that the ground was about to split open and swallow me whole at any moment. The contrast between how I felt inside and the mood of the summery festivities was incredibly jarring. While everyone around me was happily occupied with firing up the barbecue and watching some fireworks, I was quietly preoccupied with my own private world of dread.

This was quite the about-face for me—usually I'm the life of the party. But no amount of pretending could eradicate the anxiety that was gnawing at my nerves as I waited for Tuesday to roll around. I was on my way to see my gastroenterologist and was hoping to get some news. *Any* news. At that point, I just wanted someone to tell me what was wrong with my body and mind. If I knew what was wrong, I could finally start figuring out how to fix it. The effort of pretending like I was fine was absolutely exhausting. What a relief it would be to have someone lift the burden of my confusion and fear. It's like I needed someone's permission to admit that all was not well.

Little did I know just how vehement that permission would be when it finally came.

The last thing I wanted to do was worry my friends and family in the lead-up to Tuesday's meeting with my doctor. I had always been the person that others could rely on, whether they needed a shoulder to cry on or someone to get the party started. Even as I began to feel sick, I made an effort to be there for the people in my life. That Memorial Day weekend, I even kept my commitment to take part in a charity walk with my friend, despite my extreme sluggishness. I was an incredibly in-shape, seemingly healthy young person, with a longstanding personal commitment to fitness. But that charity walk, an event that should have been a breeze, had left me confined to my bed for most of the next day, too tired to move. Things that used to be easy for me were nothing short of debilitating and exhausting now.

At twenty-eight, I was a single young woman living on my own in Ohio. There was no one I had to answer to on a daily basis, no one keeping an eye on me at all times. Sure, I had friends and family I was very close with, but because I lived alone, it was easy to hide my health struggles from them. I didn't have a live-in partner or children or a roommate...well, not a *human* one, anyway. Believe it or not, it was my chihuahua, ChaCha, that kept me going as my health declined. That may seem like a heavy burden for such a little dog, but her energy and affection never wavered. If I hadn't had ChaCha to care for, I don't know how I would have kept myself engaged with the world. She was my lifeline. My anchor. Every time she let me know that she needed a walk, some food, or a snuggle, she brought me back to the world of the living. I'm convinced that she knew I needed her, too. Our pets always do.

For the most part, I was able to keep my health struggles to myself. It was important to me that no one catch on to how much trouble I was having. I'd always been driven and self-sufficient, never one to complain. I didn't want to give up my hard-won independence for anything. Even over the holiday weekend, when I was preparing myself for whatever bad news the GI might have, I kept a smile on my face. But my mom and sister, the two people who knew me best in the world, weren't buying it. They could tell that something was wrong—not just because of how I was acting, but because I was dealing with some real physical symptoms of my mystery illness. All weekend, they were conferencing between themselves, unbeknownst to me, keeping an eye on me even as I was trying to convince the rest of the world I was fine.

To be honest, I was trying to convince myself of that too.

Despite the nagging sense of doom I felt, I'd gotten dressed for my sales job that morning, same as ever. I may have been feeling sluggish and confused, but that didn't mean I was going to slack on the fashion front. I picked out a pair of flared, navy-blue pants, a white, short-sleeved, ruffled blouse, a scarf in a vibrant blue-and-green-neon leopard print, and blue patent leather heels. It was the heels that gave me pause, as I realized they barely fit anymore. My legs and feet had been swelling uncontrollably of late, and that wasn't all. When I arranged my long red hair into a neat ponytail, it felt as dry as straw in my hands—like it might snap off if I wasn't careful. Everything about my body was slightly off-kilter.

Still, I had no reason to think that anything was seriously wrong with me. I'd never had any major health problems before, and nothing like this ran in my family. My immune system had always been pretty strong—I just wasn't someone who got sick very often. I told myself as much about a million times over the course of the holiday weekend. But even the best foundation couldn't conceal the toxic undertone that had been plaguing my complexion for months. My crisp, navy-blue slacks couldn't hide the uncomfortable swelling in my legs and ankles. My polished exterior couldn't erase the aching and burning that had taken hold of my bones and muscles. My usual sunny demeanor couldn't keep my sluggishness and confusion at bay. And all the primping in the world couldn't get me out of that morning's urgent follow-up meeting with my gastroenterologist.

I'd seen my GI just the week before, in the latest installment of what felt like one long doctor's appointment that had been systematically gobbling up my entire year. I'd lost count of how many check-ups, blood tests, and ultrasounds had been ordered for me. But my GI's insistence that we see each other again so soon—not for an appointment, but a sit-down meeting—had me convinced that this wasn't going to be just another routine doctor's visit. I couldn't help but wonder why we were having a meeting instead of an appointment—what could that possibly mean? This was going to be a turning point...I just had no idea in what direction I'd be turning.

Since early 2011, I'd been experiencing a barrage of unexplainable, seemingly unrelated health issues. Though I was a young, health-conscious woman deeply committed to fitness, my endurance and energy levels had started to falter. I was having strange allergic reactions to foods that had never given me any trouble before. Just a few sips of alcohol were enough to leave me feeling quite drunk. I wasn't a heavy drinker by any means, but I was accustomed to enjoying a glass of wine or two without getting totally hammered. No matter how much sleep I got or how well and often I ate to fuel my body and mind, I still felt utterly exhausted by the middle of the day.

The disorienting rollercoaster of symptoms left me baffled and apprehensive. I could be feeling great one day and hit a brick wall of pain and exhaustion the next. My bones would start burning out of nowhere, as if they were spontaneously combusting. I'd go from eating one of my favorite foods for lunch one day to having an allergic reaction to it the next. These outlandish, random episodes left me confused about my health and frustrated that I couldn't just figure the problem out on my own. Obviously, none of this was conducive to the busy life I had built for myself in my home state. I had professional goals to conquer, business trips to take, friends to see, and family to spend time with—I couldn't afford to be slowed down like this.

At first, I tried to address this bizarre combination of symptoms on my own. Surely, I knew my body well enough to come up with a solution. I tried changing up my diet, my sleeping habits, my fitness regimen—anything to start feeling even a little bit better. But still, I couldn't shake the persistent confusion that dogged my mind, the strange texture of my hair and skin, the deep burning sensation that permeated my bones. Before long, I found myself getting lost in stores I'd frequented dozens of times. I'd find myself wandering around Kroger, my local supermarket, for hours with nothing in my cart, literally walking in circles around the place. I started to feel trapped inside a body and mind that no longer felt like my own.

Things started getting really serious when I began falling asleep in the middle of day, coming close to passing out on the job. I started walking home with a girlfriend after she found me asleep at work one afternoon, just in case something happened to me en route. I began feeling paranoid about my deteriorating state, wondering if I was cursed. One night, as my friend and I were walking home, I noticed a streetlight go out as we passed and found myself wondering if it was a sign of some impending doom.

I found myself digging into every little thing that occurred around me, every twinge and ache that went through my body. It was like reading tea leaves to try and see the future—I just wanted a way to make sense of it all, and I was starting to get desperate. Part of me wondered if I should just chalk up these strange symptoms to getting older, despite the fact that I was still in my twenties. (Leave it to a twenty-eight-year-old to think of twenty-eight as "older", right?) But as that telltale yellow tint crept across my skin, and my other symptoms started intensifying, I had to admit that something was seriously wrong.

I couldn't fix this on my own. I didn't even know what it was I needed to fix.

When my feet had swollen to the point of not being able to fit into my shoes and I found myself nearly passing out at work, I knew I'd reached a turning point. I finally bit the bullet and made a doctor's appointment. Making that first doctor's appointment to address these issues was a huge shift for me in and of itself. Admitting that I needed help, that I didn't have all the answers, was not how I was accustomed to doing things. Not by a long shot.

All my life, I'd been independent, totally in control of my own affairs. My tireless work ethic was like an engine, pushing me not just to be good enough, but to be perfect. Working hard was my escape from the nagging insecurities of the past, insecurities I'd banished to the darkest corners of my mind. Constantly striving to get ahead helped me ease the restlessness I felt living in the Midwest. I knew what I needed and how to take care of myself.

Or at least, I used to.

I certainly wasn't expecting any earth-shattering news to come out of that first doctor's appointment. I figured they'd pin my symptoms on something fairly standard—mono, perhaps—write me a prescription, and let me get on with my life. But when my first round of blood tests came back earlier that year, I had to face the fact that something was seriously, clinically off. My liver enzymes, which should have been in the low single digits, had started to spike into the thousands, and continued to creep up even further as the weeks went on.

I was completely caught off guard by the news that my health troubles had to do with my liver. I always thought that liver issues were a result of alcohol abuse—something that definitely wasn't a part of my life. Though outwardly, I was the same young, professional self-starter I'd worked so hard to become, all was not well below the surface. I went through countless rounds of blood work and ultrasounds in a very short time, all the while growing more and more exhausted. Despite the hard evidence that something was wrong with my health, I couldn't help placing the blame squarely on myself. Surely, I just wasn't trying hard enough to get better. Working hard had never failed me before. Why should this be any different?

All right, Jessica, I coached myself, starting up my car at last. *You're gonna have to stop berating yourself long enough to make it through this doctor's appointment. The second we're out of there, you can get right back to beating yourself up, I promise.*

But even as I tried to convince myself that this appointment was going to be run-of-the-mill, some part of me knew that was wishful thinking. My GI hadn't asked for a checkup, after all, but a *meeting.* Doctors only ever ask for a meeting if they have some seriously bad news to deliver. I'd seen enough medical procedural shows in my life to know *that.* But even at my most pessimistic, I couldn't have guessed just how dire my doctor's news would be when it finally came.

On May, 28, 2011, I sat silently across from my GI as our meeting unfolded, struggling to process what she was telling me. I felt like I'd been dropped into a scene from some intense dramatic movie. Moments like this didn't happen to regular people like me, surely. I clasped my hands tightly in my lap, trying to hold myself together. It felt like my mind was forcefully rejecting the doctor's words even as she spoke them. As if I could avoid my fate if I simply refused to comprehend my diagnosis.

"I need...a liver transplant?" I said softly, testing the words out for the first time.

"That's right," my GI confirmed. "Your enzyme levels have gotten worryingly high."

"But...a *transplant*?" I urged, leaning forward in my chair. "Are you sure that's really necessary? What about medication, or—"

"A transplant is absolutely necessary. There's no doubt about it," my GI replied, meeting my frantic gaze across her wide desk. "You have two choices. You can go straight to the emergency room at UC Medical Center, or you can go to Kettering Hospital and take an ambulance to Cincinnati from there. You'll meet your transplant team as soon as you get to UC."

"I...I guess I'd like to go to Kettering first?" I replied, somewhat uncertainly. I'd been to that hospital before, and right now the promise of familiarity was more compelling than anything.

"Great," my GI nodded. "We'll get you on the tristate transplant wait list right away. Then it's just a matter of finding a match."

"How long does it usually take to find a match?" I asked.

"It can vary from patient to patient," my GI replied. "But with urgent cases like yours, the wait time can be considerably shorter."

So not only was my liver damaged—it was in *urgent* distress? I felt my heart begin to race as the severity of my situation started to sink in.

"OK..." I replied, digesting the news. "How soon does this transplant need to happen? I'm sure I can schedule some time off from work if I give enough notice—"

"I'm afraid that giving notice won't be possible," my doctor told me, "You need to get medical care *immediately*, Jessica. You're going straight to the hospital from here, and you're not leaving until you've gotten a new liver."

A long moment passed as I took in her proclamation.

"But...but I have to get back to work!" I exclaimed, knowing the moment I said it that this was *not* the appropriate response.

"Well, you're just going to have to call in sick," my GI replied, laying her hand on mine. "We need to get you taken care of, Jessica. It can't wait."

I blinked up at my GI, trying to wrap my head around what was happening. Truth be told, I didn't even know what function my liver served in my body, much less what a transplant would entail. But even so, my doctor didn't need to spell it out any further for me to understand the gravity of my predicament. I could tell just by the look on her face how serious the situation was. By that point, my liver enzymes were sky high. The toxins in my body left my mouth tasting like I'd just been sucking on a penny. My body was exhausted and aching around the clock, sometimes so badly that I was paralyzed with the pain. It felt as though I'd taken to drinking battery acid that was slowly eating away at my bones. My hair was breaking off in my hands, and my legs were swollen beyond recognition. If I didn't get a transplant soon, the situation could turn lethal. It was as simple as that.

The cloud of dread that had been hovering over me all week finally burst. But the downpour of reality that washed over me didn't leave me feeling scared, or angry, as I imagined it might. Instead, what I felt was...clarity. After months of discomfort and confusion, frustration and self-recrimination, someone was finally offering me a solution. It was an extreme solution, to be sure, but I was finally getting help for what was ailing me. The peace that settled over me then was pure comfort after months of internal discord. It felt like sitting down beside a warm fire after coming in from the bitter cold. No matter what happened next, I was free from the uncertainty that had been plaguing me for the better part of a year.

And for that at least, I was grateful.

***

Chapter Two

The Road to Cincinnati

I sat in the quiet waiting room at my GI's office in Beavercreek, Ohio, doing my best to gather my reeling thoughts. There were so many things that needed to happen before I went to the hospital. Someone would need to take care of ChaCha and let my friends know what was going on. I had so many arrangements to make...and no idea where to start. Leaning forward in my chair, I glanced down and caught sight of my carefully selected work clothes. A startled gasp of disbelief escaped my lips as I remembered that I still had to call out of work...for my *liver transplant*. How's *that* for the ultimate doctor's note?

Making my way outside into the warm May afternoon, I pulled out my cell phone and punched in my boss, Sandy's, number. It wasn't just my workaholic nature that inspired me to call my boss before anyone else, and en route to the emergency room no less. Sandy was a woman I looked up to, whose opinion I trusted deeply. Even in the midst of this serious crisis, I needed her assurance that it was OK to put my health before my job.

"Of course! Take as much time as you need," Sandy told me the second I'd given her the details of my situation, "I'll be praying for you."

I'd heard the phrase, "I'll be praying for you", many

times over the course of my life. Those words had even crossed my lips more than a few times, in fact. I'd been a Catholic all my life and had offered to pray for the well-being of countless friends, family members, and neighbors over the years. To be honest though, prayer had yet to feel all that personal to me. I knew that people believed in the power of prayer, and so did I, in theory. But I had never witnessed it up close. Despite the usual setbacks and heartbreaks of childhood, adolescence, and young adulthood, nothing had ever happened in my life that called for an outpouring of prayer.

Until now, that is.

I said goodbye to Sandy and called my mom next. She was in the area and anxious to hear how the meeting with my doctor went. I told her the broad strokes of what was going on, and she immediately agreed to drive me over to the Kettering emergency room. I paced in front of the doctor's office as I waited for my mother to arrive. She would drive me from my GI's office to the ER, where we would wait together while the ICU at the University of Cincinnati Medical Center prepared a bed for me. Once I was transported and all settled in, I would meet my transplant team.

"My transplant team," I muttered, shaking my head in disbelief. It felt so bizarre to say that phrase out loud. It was like another scene from some over-the-topic medial drama—one that would probably be too melodramatic for my taste. Except this wasn't a movie; this was my *life*—the future of which was as uncertain as it had ever been.

Blinking up into the warm spring light, I tried to memorize the feeling of the sun against my skin. I had no idea how long I was going to be staying in the hospital once I got there. According to the information my GI had given me, some people could spend months or even years on the organ transplant wait list. Some part of me was still holding out hope that my liver would bounce back on its own or that this was all some crazy misunderstanding. But all the same, I did my best to absorb the outside world, save it up while I could.

Call it my sensory insurance policy.

I looked over to see my mom pulling into the parking lot of my GI's office. Her short brunette bob, so distinct from my long red locks, caught my eye through the windshield. As we locked eyes through the glass, her expression was as composed and determined as ever. My mom's many years of working as a nurse had prepared her for any crisis, and I knew she expected me to be ready as well. I made my way over to her car, trying to hold my head high even as my bones and muscles ached with every single step I took. I'd been fighting with my exhausted body for months, urging it hurry on up. But now, as I settled into the passenger seat beside my mom, I finally felt that I could cut my tired body some slack. I wish it hadn't taken a major health crisis to get me to sit still for a minute...but all the same, I was happy for the rest.

I didn't say much as we drove along, but my silence wasn't one of misery or woe. Instead, I was basking in a brand-new feeling of relief. The bizarre aches and mysterious allergic reactions that had been plaguing my body finally made sense. My pain wasn't just in my head, the result of me being unduly hard on myself. What was really happening to me was so much bigger than that. But as I'd find out later, my health troubles weren't totally unrelated to my lifelong habit of being too hard on myself. As it turned out, my tendency to strive for perfection had done me much more harm than good.

I'd spent a sizable chunk of my young life either on the move or staring myself down in the mirror...often at the same time. As a girl, I was a serious dancer, devoting hours upon hours of every week to honing my craft. Every moment I wasn't in school, I was practicing, rehearsing, or performing. I would line up in the studio alongside my fellow dancers, facing a wall of floor-to-ceiling mirrors as we went through our various routines. I loved the precision and discipline of dance, the way I could train my body to move exactly the way I wanted. But at the same time, all those hours in front of the mirror had an impact on how I saw myself. I couldn't help but compare my body to those of my fellow dancers, resenting the imperfections I saw (or imagined) in my own form. And as unpleasant as these reactions were, the satisfaction that came with fixing my supposed "imperfections" was unmatched and nothing short of addicting.

As a bright, ambitious, small-town girl, I knew that I needed to work hard to achieve my big city dreams. From the time I was small, I knew I wasn't destined to live in the Midwest all my life. I knew that I wanted more excitement and energy than my home state could offer, and for a time, I thought dance would be my ticket to bigger and better things. Maybe I could become a background dancer—or better yet, a Rockette. Dance provided me with an immediate, physical outlet for my striving determination. No matter what other pressures or obligations were weighing on me, there was always something I could focus on and perfect in the dance studio.

My passion for dance was profound and expansive. I couldn't get enough. Ballet, jazz, pointe, modern; I wanted to conquer it all. I had an inextinguishable drive to keep moving, and to the people around me, that drive must have seemed admirable. But my dedication to my craft masked a darker side of my ambition. As much as I loved to dance, there was always a nasty little voice in my head, telling me that my hard work would never be enough. I would never be perfect. Dance became less about enjoying the movement my body was capable of and more about punishing my body instead. As a young girl, I didn't have the self-esteem to appreciate myself exactly as I was. My self-worth was completely bound up in how others saw and reacted to me, and being a dancer was a big part of the image I presented to the world.

To me, being a dancer was elite and exclusive. Dancers were disciplined and driven, classy and enviable. Dancers were sexy, skinny, and highly skilled. Dancers were everything a girl could ever want to be, though few would make the cut. I realized by the time I was a teenager that I was never going to be the best dancer out there. I was technically proficient but didn't have that spark that truly gifted dancers possess. I'd lost it somewhere along the way—probably while I was otherwise occupied with hating my body. I couldn't change that limiting fact, but I could change everything else about me. If I wasn't going to be the best dancer, I was going to be the skinniest. The prettiest. The closest to perfect. What I couldn't achieve on the toes of my pointe shoes, I'd achieve by restricting my diet and whittling my waist down to nothing.

Looking back, it's easy for me to recognize my extreme behaviors around food and exercise as an eating disorder. But awareness about eating disorders was not as widespread back then as it is today. To the people around me, I was just an active young girl who happened to eat like a bird. But in reality, I was trying to build up my sense of self by diminishing my body as much as possible. I was so busy comparing myself to the perfect women I saw on TV and in the pages of magazines that I never learned to appreciate the wonderful, healthy body I'd been blessed with. Young women are always being told that they're not enough. And I, like so many others, believed that lie for a very long time.

After sixteen years of hard work, I had to acknowledge that I wasn't going to dance professionally. By the time I was a young adult, dance had become more about controlling my body than about joyful expression and art. But after relying on dance as an outlet for my anxieties and insecurities for so long, I was terrified of what my life would look like without it. Soon, I found other containers for my devotion to form, fitness, and discipline. As an adult, I became interested in fitness competitions, finessing every inch of my body for these events with extensive training. As a control-loving perfectionist, the satisfaction I got from this regimen was downright euphoric. I could spend hours upon hours focused on one small area of my body, sculpting it to my ideal specifications. No matter how busy I was with work, friends, and family, I always found plenty of time to devote to the gym.

It wasn't just my workout schedule that became more extreme during that time, either. My diet underwent a massive transformation as well. Though I'd always been a pretty healthy eater, I found myself replacing an increasing number of my meals with protein shakes and supplements. There was a science to dieting, and I loved that aspect of it. But somehow, it didn't occur to me that I was treating my body like a science experiment—something entirely removed from myself. That kind of dissociation is common

21

in people with eating disorders, but nobody around me thought anything was amiss. And why would they? We're all conditioned to think that the best thing a woman can be is thin, and that thinness is the same as healthiness.

Well, I can tell you from experience that that's not even *remotely* true.

Even as I worked my body ever closer to perfection, I couldn't deny that this lifestyle was unsustainable in the long run. As hard as I trained, the horizon of perfection kept receding. There was always another millimeter of fat that could be burned away, another muscle group that needed further toning. And while I was working hard to shape and strengthen my exterior, it was becoming harder to listen to what my body was really asking for. At the height of my fitness obsession, I found myself sitting with my legs elevated to increase the blood flow to my glutes while eating one dry scoop of protein powder. As a *meal*. If not that's being disconnected from what your body actually needs and wants, I don't know what is.

Ultimately, I realized that my passion and goal-oriented nature were just as useful in the workplace as in the gym and dance studio. While I always kept up with my health and fitness, I dove into my sales career with the full force of my determination. Though I loved being close to my family and tight-knit group of friends in Ohio, I'd always wanted to travel beyond the borders of my home state. I wanted to see the rest of the country—the rest of the *world*—and I knew that a career in sales could make that happen.

I always knew that I was meant to live somewhere else, far beyond the borders of Ohio. Growing up, I daydreamed constantly about what my life would look like when I was all grown up. I pictured a glamorous, modern studio apartment in some big city, with ballet bars around the perimeter and mirror-lined walls. I imaged a pristine concrete floor that I could spend hours dancing across. No matter where I moved, who I met, or what experiences came my way, life in Ohio was just never enough for me. It was like I was homesick for a place I hadn't even seen yet. I could sense that there was somewhere in the world that would finally feel like home, but I just didn't know where it was.

By the time I was twenty-eight, I was well on my way to having the career and life I'd always wanted. As a sales professional, I traveled everywhere from Atlanta to Las Vegas for my job. Sooner or later, I was bound to discover the place I truly belonged. My sales territory at that time covered entire swaths of Ohio, Kentucky, and Indiana. Slowly but surely, I was venturing farther away from Dayton, Ohio—the only home I had ever known. I knew the major highways like the back of my hand, after countless hours of crisscrossing them as I traveled to meet with potential clients.

But for all my familiarity with those roads, I never expected to be riding along one of them in the back of an ambulance.

I felt surprisingly calm as I was transported from the Kettering ER to the medical center in Cincinnati, where my transplant team was assembling. After months of trying and inevitably failing to heal myself through sheer force of will, there was nothing for me to do now but lie on a gurney and wait. I'd expended so much effort trying to power through life as my liver grew weaker. It was a relief, placing myself in someone else's hands for once. I trusted the medical professionals at UC, the family and friends who were waiting in the wings to support me. And above all, I trusted God—even if I didn't fully know what that meant yet.

I'd grown up in a religious household, surrounded by people with a deep understanding of what it meant to have faith. But as I reached my late twenties, I was questioning the nature of my own relationship with faith. What did it even mean to *have* faith, anyway? I was so restless, so uncertain about the path my life was supposed to take that I couldn't help but wonder about the plan God had in store for me. It felt like I was still searching, still wandering aimlessly at that point in my life. How could there be a path for me if I didn't even know where it started?

What I would learn soon enough is that you can't always see the path stretching out before you—but that doesn't mean it isn't there. You have to be patient as you wait to understand the ways in which God is working in your life. Only with the patience that comes with trusting His plan can you really live in the moment. I wish I had known that in my twenties, instead of always rushing ahead to the next thing. God reveals things to us when we need to know them and not a moment sooner. In my illness, God was already beginning to reveal some big truths about my life, my destiny, and my faith.

And He was just getting started.

Glancing through the back windows of the ambulance, I watched as the familiar landscape trundled by. Out of the corner of my eye, I spotted a sign for Interstate 75—an infamously traffic-ridden stretch of Ohio highway that I knew all too well. I'd spent far too many hours of my life bumper-to-bumper with other commuters on this very road. And with the rate at which my liver function was declining, I found myself seriously wondering if I was going to die before we reached the UC Medical Center.

I've got to say, though, that would be some coroner's report: Jessica Steck. Age twenty-eight. Cause of death, traffic on I-75.

As fate would have it, traffic was surprisingly light that day, and we made good time on our way to Cincinnati. As the familiar landmarks of the city came into view, a million happy memories came flooding into my mind's eye. Cincinnati was "the City" to the residents of my small hometown. For me, a trip to Cincinnati meant shopping with my girlfriends, hanging out at a favorite bar or restaurant, and family outings with my parents and younger siblings. At twenty-eight, I should have been heading into the city for an afternoon of mani-pedis with my girls or for a first date with a new love interest—not for a liver transplant.

But then, nothing about this situation should have been happening. As I was wheeled into the ICU, I had to leave my "shoulds" and "supposed tos" at the door. I would accept whatever happened to me once I entered the hospital.

What else was there to do?

***

Chapter Three

Waiting and Hoping

As if from outside myself, I watched as a dozen medical professionals buzzed around me, setting me up for my stay in Room 1 in the intensive care unit. I met my liver transplant team right away and was amazed at just how many people it was going to take to get me back into good health. My body needed to be stabilized, my liver damage assessed. Machines were wheeled in to stand vigil at my bedside as nurses adorned me with countless wires and tubes. Through the hectic, bustling activity going on all around me, I heard someone mutter that my liver function was at a dizzyingly low 20 percent. Getting me hooked up to an IV was a trial in itself, as my veins kept bursting at the slightest touch. I looked on with silent awe as the gravity of my situation was reflected back to me in the faces of my medical team.

"I don't know how you got out of bed this morning, given how sick you are," one of the doctors on my transplant team told me. "You're lucky to be alive."

Hearing that straight from my doctor's mouth left me shaken. I realized as my medical team got me settled into my room that this was the real deal. If I'd waited any longer to seek treatment, it may have been too late. I'd put off getting help for so long as it was—my pride and need to be totally independent could have been the end of me. In the face of that grave realization, one thought ran across my mind in an endless loop.

I need my family.

As the oldest of three kids, I grew up knowing that it was my responsibility to set a good example for my younger brother and sister. It was my job to lend a hand when my parents needed help with the littler kids, to put on a brave face in times of stress, to be as self-reliant as possible to lighten the load for everyone else. My mom also came from a family of three children, where everyone was expected to pitch in as soon as they were able. And for my dad, one of four growing up in the country, it meant that everyone in his family knew what it meant to pull their weight, too. To me, being the oldest child meant handling my own problems, keeping my private life to myself, and protecting my little siblings as best I could.

But the second I found myself in the ICU, all those noble eldest sister aims went right out the window. I couldn't protect my parents and siblings from the reality of what was happening to me. My mom and sister had already begun to suspect that something was wrong, and now they knew it for sure. And even if I wanted to try and shield them, I knew they wouldn't stand for it. We may have never been a sentimental family, but we were nothing if not fiercely loyal. There was no way my family was going to let me go through this alone.

When I first caught a glimpse of them through the glass windows of my hospital room, I had to wonder if they were some kind of hallucination. I'd been praying for them to appear, and there they were—as if I'd conjured them up myself. One by one, I watched as my parents and siblings filed into my room in the ICU, taking in the sight of me in my bed for the first time. Though they were each already in action mode and keeping their emotions in check, they couldn't hide the mistiness in their eyes as they spotted the tubes and wires protruding from my arms, the wall of machines circling my bed. My landing in the hospital was a complete surprise, and no one had had time to prepare for it. But despite their distress, my family never let me know just how worried they were. Especially not my mother.

"All right," Mom said, turning to address the rest of my family like a commanding officer doling out orders to her troops. "Here's what we're gonna do..."

Mom took charge straightaway, as the person with the most medical know-how and a knack for keeping calm under pressure. She fell into step easily with the doctors and nurses around us, and they accepted her into their ranks without question. They must have recognized in her the unflappable, matter-of-fact nature that is necessary for survival in the nursing profession. Even in my diminished state, I felt a sense of pride at my mom's masterful handling of our family's crisis.

As a kid, it was sometimes hard to understand Mom's

practical, straightforward approach to emotional subjects. We never really went in for the typical mother-daughter chats about my personal life—my friends and crushes, all the usual girlhood dramas. The *Gilmore Girls*, we were not. Instead, my mom focused on pushing me to do my best in all things, making sure I was living up to the tremendous potential she saw in all her children. Having married my dad, Tom, at the young age of twenty-two and moved out of her familiar city surroundings to start a family with him in the country, my mom was absolutely devoted to us kids. Our relationship may not have been warm and fuzzy at all times, but Mom was there for me when it counted. And that first night in the ICU was no exception.

My sister, Rebecca, five years my junior, became my mom's right-hand woman from the moment I landed in the hospital. A teacher by trade and temperament, Rebecca made herself my de facto social media manager, keeping my close-knit circle of friends informed of my status through a massive group text chain. Mom would gather information from the doctors and nurses and translate it into layman's terms for Rebecca, who would then pass what she knew along to my friends. In no time at all, my practical, resourceful mom and sister had worked out a system of communication all their own. And good thing, too—by then, I was way past of the point of being able to contribute much in the way of strategy.

At the time of my hospitalization, I was romantically

unattached. The main men in my life were still my dad and little brother, David. They were more than ready to take on the physical, everyday tasks that I needed help with as I waited and hoped—either for a transplant to come through or for my liver to miraculously get better all by itself. I didn't even know that the liver *could* regenerate itself. It was surreal, getting so intimately acquainted with this part of my body that I'd never thought about before in my life. It made me realize just how little time I'd spent thinking about my body beyond my external appearance.

I'll never forget the sudden tears that sprung into my father's eyes the moment he saw me lying in that hospital bed. The gentleness with which David—who was only twenty-one—helped me eat when I could no longer feed myself. The selflessness of my mom and sister as they made sure everyone else was OK. I believe that real strength is in being able to see someone in their most vulnerable state and being able to be there for them without falling to pieces.

And by that metric, my parents and siblings are the strongest people I know.

For those first few days in the ICU, all we could do was wait and see. My doctors had only one job for me to do, which was eat as much as possible. It was strange for me to suddenly be tasked with eating everything and anything I could, given how restrictively healthy my diet had been in the past. After years of being vigilant about never eating junk food, I was eating what felt like my body weight in candy. It became clear just how unaccustomed I was to sweets when I nearly choked to death on a Starburst...but then again, that kind of thing is bound to happen when you have all manner of tubes running down your throat.

I'd been placed on the tristate transplant wait list, and my doctors were doing their best to keep me healthy enough to even be eligible for a new liver. At any given point, more than one hundred thousand Americans are waiting for organ transplants. And on average, twenty-two people die each day while waiting for a transplant. The system that determines who will receive the organ they so desperately need runs according to a complex, ever-shifting set of factors. These factors include how severely ill someone is, the time they've spent on the waitlist, their blood type, and whether the host's body is likely to accept the new organ.

As a young, healthy woman, I'd spent just about no time at all on this list considering the inner workings of the national organ transplant network. I knew about the importance of organ donation, sure. But I had no idea what kept the system working, or that up to eight lives could be saved or improved by the grace of one single organ donor. At that age, I was so completely occupied with my career, my social life, and my ambitions that I never paused to consider what would happen if I myself were in need of an organ transplant. What twentysomething would? As I was placed on the tristate wait list, my entire life had come to depend on a system I knew next to nothing about to replace an organ

I knew next to nothing about.

Luckily, whether or not I received a new liver wouldn't come down to a quiz.

Despite the severity of my illness, my doctors were still leaving room for hope that my liver would recover on its own. It was a long shot, but they weren't ruling anything out during that first leg of my time in the ICU. In the meantime, though, there was little that could be done to keep me comfortable. Because my liver wasn't functioning correctly, my body wasn't able to process medication. Any medicine administered to me would just become another toxin my system couldn't handle, going straight to my already overtaxed brain. This meant that anesthesia or any kind of painkillers were out of the question. I could feel everything for the duration of my treatment—even throughout the various tests that needed to be run on me.

When my doctors performed a biopsy, I could feel the tube as it snaked through my entire body. They threaded the tube through a hole they'd made on either side of my neck, which is not exactly standard protocol. Typically, a biopsy is run through one's side, but that—like anesthesia—was out of the question for me. I was at too great a risk of heavy bleeding for the normal biopsy procedure to be used. I felt the entirety of my stress test as well, an experience that nothing could have prepared me for. It amounted to a stifling, suffocating panic that I won't soon forget. I'd never felt pain like this in my life—but I'd feel plenty more before this ordeal was over.

I badly craved the simple comforts of self-care during that time. What I wouldn't have given for a nice, long bubble bath and a full-body massage. I was so desperate to feel normal that I would drag myself into the bathroom to shower and brush my teeth, despite my body's protestations. I wasn't even allowed to shave my legs, I was at such a high risk of heavy bleeding. One nick of the razor, and I could have bled to death on the bathroom floor. Another thing I never knew about my liver was that it was responsible for clotting my blood, and without it, I couldn't take the risk of getting even a single scratch.

It probably goes without saying, but none of this was my idea of a good time.

I was determined to stay positive during those long, initial days of waiting. Even as the days and nights started to blur together, there was still hope that my liver might make a recovery, even if that hope was slim. My family and friends were sacrificing so much of their time, energy, and love to be with me during those trying days. I wanted them to see that I was hopeful, that I was ready to fight. I knew that seeing me in that bed, with tubes trailing from my arms and all manner of tests being administered to my ailing body, was incredibly hard for them. The least I could do was try and keep my spirits up, not just for their sake, but for my own.

At first, no one spoke a word about just how sick I

actually was—how very close to death I was. We were all staying hopeful, leaning on the power of prayer to help me recover. In my mind, I was still hanging in there, doing pretty well given the circumstances. I had no idea just how grim the situation really was, and I'm not sure I would have wanted to know from the get-go. Focusing on the incredible outpouring of love from my family and friends, the kindness of my doctors and nurses, the fact that I could still talk and visit with people, was a much brighter place for my mind to dwell.

Even if I wasn't always entirely aware of what was going on, just spending time with my friends and family was vitally nourishing. Though I, like everyone else I know, was majorly addicted to my cell phone, I never once noticed its absence while I was in the hospital. It was hard enough to stay present to the people who were actually in front of me—I wouldn't have been able to handle the additional stress of wrangling my online social circle. The people who came to see me took my mind off my illness, and their prayers made me feel hopeful. If I'd known how sick I was from the start, it may have been harder to have hope. And hope can be a pretty invaluable medicine, especially when more traditional treatments are off the table.

But before long, we'd run out of time to wait and see. It became clear that there was no miraculous recovery on the way for my failing liver. I couldn't be kept out of the loop any longer, as hard decisions needed to be made.

Hard questions needed to be asked, too. In the run-up to my transplant, I was made to account for my entire medical history and grilled about my lifestyle choices. People have certain assumptions about those who suffer from liver failure, often jumping to conclusions about drug and alcohol abuse. And while I'd never used drugs or abused alcohol, I still felt like I was being interrogated about my every habit. On my fifth day in the ICU, one of the staff GIs starting doling out the point-blank truths.

"The fact of the matter is, you're lucky to still be alive," the doctor told me, as gently as he could. "At this point, your liver is about 40 percent dead, basically without function. I'm surprised it hasn't given out entirely, given the shape it's in. One quarter of this damage would have been alarming in itself, but *this*...?"

"So, it's not going to get better," I said drowsily, letting this fact sink in.

"You're going to need a new liver," the doctor continued earnestly, as my family and friends exchanged somber looks across my hospital bed. "And you're going to need one *soon*."

***

Chapter Four

Getting By with a Little Help from My Friends

By my late twenties, I had formed a close, fiercely devoted circle of friends who were as much my family as those who shared my blood. Like many people of my generation, I'd come to rely on my friends as sources of comfort and strength as I set off into my adult life. Having a group of people my own age who were facing the same challenges and struggles I was encountering made the transition into adulthood much less daunting. My friends were as involved and invested in my life as I was in theirs, and my hospital room may as well have had a revolving door as they all came to check in on me in shifts.

Though patients awaiting organ donations aren't permitted to have flowers—or anything else that could contaminate the transplant process—my friends would not be deterred in their efforts to cheer me up. Entire mountain ranges of stuffed animals began accumulating in my room. My girlfriends would arrive with nail polish in tow, determined to keep me feeling pampered as we waited to see if I would pull through. One of my sister's friends had even sent me a medicine bottle filled with holy water, acquired and blessed on a recent trip to Bethlehem, which I took precious sips from in a desperate effort to heal myself.

By then, I was willing to try anything. My friends were a constant, comforting presence during that time of uncertainty, just as they were in every other phase of my life.

I was so grateful to my friends for being there when I needed them, but we all had to admit that this was a pretty crazy reversal of roles for me within our group. For as long as any of us could remember, I was the designated up-for-anything friend in our circle. I lived my life in a constant state of motion and was always ready to jump onboard for a last-minute party, vacation, or road trip. I was always pushing myself to say *yes* whenever possible, never thinking too hard about the consequences or fallout.

I started to wonder, as I sat in that hospital bed, if there was a reason why I had always gone about my life this way. Had some part of me known that my time on this planet was drastically limited? That would explain the little fire inside of me that always kept me moving, that wouldn't let me pass up an opportunity for a new, exciting experience. Maybe I'd been compelled to fit as much fun and enjoyment into my first twenty-eight years of life because twenty-eight years was all I had? I'd always justified my spontaneous nature by declaring that "life is short!" But I hadn't had any idea just how short it might actually be.

Though I had plenty of friends visiting me in the ICU, that didn't stop me from making a few more along the way. During my stay at UC, I was attended to by an incredible team of nurses, many of whom were my age. While my doctors were figuring out a big-picture plan for my care, my incredible nurses were right by my side, helping me with the small, everyday tasks that kept me feeling like myself. Even though I was deathly ill, my nurses never treated me like I was "just a patient." When they looked at me, they didn't see my sickness—they saw their peer. A girl they could very well find themselves at a party with outside the hospital walls. No matter how ill I became, my nurses never treated me like a diagnosis.

And in a way, that was the best medicine they could have given me.

"Ugh, you don't wanna come near me," I slurred, shaking my head as a couple of nurses appeared in my doorway. "I smell like shit over here!"

The corners of the nurses' mouths twitched upward as I swore away with abandon. As my sickness progressed, I was beginning to act more and more like a drunken sailor. That's because I was literally becoming intoxicated by way of my own body. My eyes and skin had taken on a jaundiced, yellow hue. My ammonia levels were creeping upward, altering my brain function and making me act disoriented— *and* disorderly. I couldn't believe the vulgar language that flew so uncharacteristically out of my mouth—but that didn't stop us from getting a kick out of it.

"Listen to this one," my mom tutted, with mock disapproval. "You're lucky you're so sick—otherwise we'd be washing your mouth out with soap!"

I wasn't the only one who'd become friendly with the nursing staff. My mom was a kindred spirit of these younger nurses, falling into step with them from the start. They recognized my mom as one of their own. She knew how to speak their language, after all. How to keep things as light as possible for the sake of everyone's sanity, no matter how heavy our hearts became. In my room, the nurses could be themselves, treat me like one of the gang. With her connection to both me and the nurses, my mom made a full circuit out of us all.

"You know what I would kill for? A slushie," I went on absentmindedly, staring up at the ceiling that had become as familiar to me as the inside of my eyelids. "A *lemon* slushie."

"We'll see what we can do about that, just as soon as we've got you back in working order," one of the nurses said, winking, giving me a supportive pat on the thigh before commencing with what felt like my millionth round of blood work.

I was constantly distracted from my waiting by an endless stream of tests, checkups, and consultations. It wasn't just my doctors and nurses always stopping by to take some blood or measure my ammonia levels. When you're waiting and hoping for an organ transplant, you find yourself meeting with all manner of supportive professionals. They don't just give a new organ to anybody. They need to be confident that you understand the incredible gift you're receiving and the responsibility that goes into taking care of it. An organ transplant means a second chance at life—and no one wants to see that chance go to waste.

I was visited by social workers, dietitians, and pharmacists. I even met with a financial planner, who wanted to help me make a plan for shouldering the burden of the medical bills I was sure to rack up in this process. I couldn't believe how many people were committed to helping me through this massive transition in my life...but I couldn't help but wonder all the while if their kind efforts would be for nothing.

As light and breezy as everyone was trying to keep things, it was impossible to ignore my worsening condition. If I had been in my right mind, it would have horrified me to have all these people see me slurring my words, unable to bathe or eat or on my own. The swelling that had started in my ankles and legs was spreading throughout my entire body. Back when I'd first started noticing my symptoms, I was annoyed that my swelling feet would no longer fit in my extensive collection of shoes—my most beloved guilty pleasure as a shopper. Now, my entire body was ballooning to the point where I could barely recognize myself, but I was far too concerned about slipping into a coma to give my weight much thought.

Turns out that the view from death's door will do wonders for your perspective.

Chapter Five

A Turn for the Worse

My chest ached with tightness as I struggled to catch my breath. I'd just returned from trying to use the bathroom, a task which, by then, had become a grueling ordeal. The room spun around me as I sank heavily onto the edge of my hospital bed, flanked as ever by my mom and sister. I glanced around the room that had become my entire world, unable to remember what day it was or even what *time* of day it was. My thoughts slipped through my fingers as I tried to grab hold of them, like so many grains of sand. When I finally brought my gaze up to meet my mother's, I could feel tears beginning to prick my eyes.

"Mom..." I whispered, barely able to focus on her face. "I...I think I'm losing it."

"It's OK, honey. You're doing great," she said encouragingly.

I couldn't help but complete the unspoken second half of her statement in my mind: *"...for someone who's dying."*

"What can we do?" my sister asked, brushing a greasy, tangled lock of hair away from my forehead. It had been days since I'd showered last, and I could feel a film of dirtiness covering my body. The hair on my legs was getting so out of control, I'd need a lawn mower to tame it when the time came. *If* the time came.

"I feel like...I can't hold on to my body...?" I said, my words running together as I looked between my mom and sister, hoping they would understand me. The way their expressions darkened at my words, I knew they could hear what I was trying to tell them. I was beginning to feel my grip on this world loosen. It felt for the life of me like I was beginning to drift away.

"When was the last time you were able to urinate?" my mom asked sharply, taking a hard left into nurse mode as she examined my swollen body.

"I'm not sure...I couldn't, just before," I muttered, scanning her face for any hint of distress. "Is that bad?"

"What about eating? Swallowing?" she pressed. I shook my head in response, and her mouth settled into a hard, straight line.

"Mom... What is it?" Rebecca asked, noticing the shift in my mom's demeanor.

"Wait with your sister," Mom replied. "I'll be right back."

And with that, she turned on her heel on marched out of my room, taking matters into her own hands, as ever. Rebecca sat down on the edge of my bed, adjusting the pillows behind my head for the umpteenth time. My back ached from long days of being bedridden. I couldn't believe I'd gotten to the point where simply lying down was painful.

"Dad's got everyone we've ever met praying for you," she told me, without exaggeration. "And plenty of people we've never met, too. It's wild, Jess. People all over the world are praying for you right this second."

"I know..." I replied, distracted by the huge effort of trying to swallow.

"What do you mean, you know?" Rebecca asked, studying my face.

"I can feel them," I told her adamantly. "Their prayers."

I knew that I sounded loopy, trying to describe the sensation that had settled over me as I waited in the ICU. Since the moment I learned that I needed to be hospitalized, people had been telling me that they intended to pray for me. At first, I thought of these sentiments as simple kind gestures. "I'll pray for you" was, to me, just something you said to someone in need. Like "get well soon" or "feel better." I'd been raised in a Christian household but had never experienced firsthand the difference that prayer can make in a moment of crisis—the real, physical sensation of comfort it can grant you. I never understood the true power of prayer until I found myself in great need of it.

But as my stay in the hospital stretched on, and my prognosis became more grim, I started to truly *feel* the outpouring of prayer from my friends, family, and even passing acquaintances. Though I had every reason to be frightened about the outcome of my illness, I didn't feel a lick of fear as the days wore on. Instead, I felt a mighty calm settle over me, like a warm quilt wrapping around my ailing body. Knowing that people around the world were praying for me didn't just give me hope, it activated my faith in a way I had never experienced before.

In the years before I got sick, I admit that my faith had been resting on the back burner of my life. My twenties were a time of great transition and change for me, as they are for most young people. I was discovering my professional potential, my goals and ambitions in life, and what I was truly capable of. I was questioning everything, seeking new answers at every turn. No aspect of my life went unconsidered during those whirlwind years, including my faith. I had to ask myself the hard questions about what I believed, what role God would play in my life going forward. To be honest, I hadn't been able to fully answer those questions on my own. Not until I found myself in the ICU, on the receiving end of an incredible, life-changing cascade of prayer.

"Hey..." I muttered, catching a glimpse of my sister's concerned expression. "Don't you go feeling scared for me."

"You don't have to be the big sister right now," Rebecca replied, smiling softly. "You're allowed to take a break once in a while."

"It's not that..." I went on, struggling to put my words in the right order, "It's just...*I'm* not afraid, so why should you have to be?"

46

"You really don't feel the least bit scared..." she said. It was more of an observation than a question.

"No," I confirmed. "Because nothing is happening to me that isn't supposed to happen. I know I can trust that, now."

After spending so much of my life beating myself up for not being perfect, second-guessing my decisions, and striving to do better, finding this trust was a revelation. Relieved of the obligation to control every aspect of my life, I could step back and let God take the lead. I could gaze back along the path my life had taken and realize that it had unfolded in exactly the way it needed to.

My constant adjusting and worrying hadn't changed a thing about my outcome, they'd only distracted me from being fully in the moment along the way. I'd wasted so much time and energy striving to *appear* happy instead of actually *being* happy. I'd masked my frantic soul-searching with superficial distractions. Finally, at what might be the last leg of my journey in this life, I knew that I hadn't been traveling alone after all. God had been there every step of the way, as he would continue to be now. My life was in his hands. All at once, the clarity I'd been chasing down for years had finally arrived. I'd only needed to stop moving long enough for it to catch up with me.

My sister and I glanced up as my mom reentered the room, a handful of medical professionals on her heels.

"Your mom tells us you're having some trouble," one of my doctors said, getting ready to examine me. "Let's see what's going on."

What was going on, it turned out, was that my ammonia levels had skyrocketed. Ammonia is usually excreted through one's urine, but because I was no longer able to go to the bathroom properly, my body was retaining the toxin. The ammonia levels in my blood were easily four times the normal amount for healthy adults. At this rate, my brain could be permanently damaged, and my intoxicated behavior could escalate from benignly silly to dangerously out of control. I had taken a serious turn for the worse. One that I might not come back from.

***

Chapter Six

A Close Call

Pondering the specifics of one's own funeral can be a bizarre experience in the most neutral of circumstances. Making calm, rational decisions about what flowers, music, and readings you'd prefer for your big send-off are sure to inspire some complicated feelings, no matter the setting. But if you're really looking for a trip, try thinking through your funeral arrangements while drunk on your own blood supply on the anniversary of your grandfather's death. I promise, it's an experience you won't soon forget.

My mom and sister were remarkably calm as we all sat down to get my affairs in order. They'd taken to approaching my illness with frank pragmatism, treating it like any other problem that needed to be solved. They spent hours in the hospital library, researching liver failure and toxicity, as if the right set of answers were all we needed to get through this mess. They were fully committed to doing their part in this struggle, believing all the while that they'd find a way to save me...even as we started to plan my funeral.

As I did my best to weigh the merits of lilies versus carnations as funeral flowers, my mind kept wandering away. More specifically, it kept wandering back along my lineage. I couldn't help but reflect on the members of my family who had come before me, perhaps because my place on the family tree was in danger of becoming permanently truncated. Above all, my two grandfathers occupied my thoughts that day; Grandpa Charlie, who had passed away four years ago, and Grandpa Marion, who was still emphatically with us and one of the strongest, humblest men I'd ever known.

"Huh…" I murmured, letting my head roll to the side of my pillow. "That's weird…"

"What is, honey?" my mom asked, looking up from the notes she was taking about my memorial preferences.

"Grandpa Marion… He might just outlive me," I replied, my eyes going wide with this latest revelation.

"We don't know that," my sister cut in, sitting across the room with her face buried in her phone as she scrambled to update my circle of friends about my nose-diving condition.

The toxins in the blood had crept steadily upward as the days went by. My doctors were doing their best to control the rise, but there was only so much they could do. My liver was dying, and a match had yet to be found. If my failing organ couldn't hold out until a replacement became available, there was nothing more that could be done. I'd die of liver failure here in my room at UC. That's precisely why I insisted on getting my last wishes down on paper that day—I simply didn't know how many more days I had left.

"What do you think you would like to be wearing?" my

mom asked me, pulling my attention back to the task at hand.

"Wearing?" I asked, having forgotten what we were talking about.

"At the funeral," my mom reminded me.

It was gentler than saying *In your casket* I suppose.

I pondered the question as my audience of machines chirped and hummed all around me. In a matter of days, I'd gone from picking out an outfit for work to picking out what clothes I wanted to be buried in. It had only been a week since my meeting with my GI in Beavercreek. And now here I was, trying to nail down what I wanted to be wearing in my casket.

"Oh! I know," I said suddenly, latching onto a passing thought. "I should be wearing jeans...the cute distressed ones, you know?"

"Jeans?" my sister asked, looking up in surprise from the group text.

"Yeah," I said with as much enthusiasm as I could muster. "Jeans...and my old pointe shoes...and a plain white T-shirt."

My mom and sister traded skeptical glances across the room. I had never really been what you'd call a "jeans and T-shirt girl" before. I had a soft spot for shopping and fashion, with my particular weakness being shoes. I used to head into Cincinnati with my girlfriends or my sister, spending entire days trying on the latest styles and trends. My sales job allowed me to dress up a bit for work, and I loved styling myself with care and precision. I was proud of the wardrobe I'd built up. It helped me feel like the big-city career woman I'd always aspired to be, even as a small-town girl. Safe to say, jeans and a white T-shirt would not be anyone's first guess of what I'd like to be buried in.

"That *can't* be your final answer," my mom said, eyebrows raised.

"What made you think of jeans and a white T-shirt?" Rebecca asked.

"Grandpa Marion," I said, as if it were the most obvious thing in the world. "When I think of him, that's what he's wearing...jeans and a white T-shirt."

All throughout my childhood, I'd had ambitions of leaving my sleepy little town behind and living a successful, jet-setting life. That drive had propelled me through high school, college, and into my burgeoning sales career. I'd fit a lot of striving into a relatively short life, seeing more of the world than many people in my hometown could ever dream of.

But now, as I was considering that this might very well be the end of my life, I felt my attachment to glamour and success start to fade away. I didn't need to be perceived as different or better than the people I grew up with, the people

I came from. They were good, hardworking people, dedicated to their families and communities. Just because I didn't want to live in Ohio for the rest of my life didn't mean that I had to define myself in opposition to the people who did. Suddenly, it seemed to me that there was nothing more honorable than being seen, finally, as the farmer's daughter I really was.

"Well then...jeans and a T-shirt it is," Mom said softly, dutifully writing down my unexpected response.

"Oh, and Rebecca..." I went on, inspired by another sudden thought. "You should have all my clothes, OK?"

"Now I *know* you're not in your right mind," she said, a surprised laugh escaping her lips.

Though we were five years apart in age, Rebecca and I grew up locked in constant battle over the contents of each other's closets. Like most sisters, we were always borrowing each other's stuff (with or without permission), bartering for better goods, and swapping items until it was hard to say what belonged to whom. Handing my entire wardrobe over to Rebecca was, in a sense, the biggest symbolic expression of sisterly love I could offer. And she knew it full well, too.

"I'm serious," I told her, struggling to focus on her face. "I want you to have everything."

"Well, I'm gonna hold you to that once you're better," Rebecca said, refusing to let her spirits waver, even in the face of grave uncertainty.

My eyes began to cloud over with tears as I looked between my mom and sister. There was so much I wanted to say to them, and I hated the fact that I wasn't coherent enough to put all my thoughts into words. I knew that my death my imminent, by then. But as much as I wanted to communicate clearly and deeply with my friends and family, stringing together the simplest of sentences was as much as I could manage. Would my last words really be some drunken, rambling tangent? Being robbed of my bodily autonomy was one thing, but not having full control over my own mind was just as bad. It felt like a betrayal.

And the mutiny had only just begun.

As the day went on in Room 1 of the ICU, all hell broke loose within my body. The floodgates had opened inside me, and my system was completely overrun with toxins. The world swam before my eyes, a chaotic blur of color and noise. My medical team sprang into action, mobilizing to bring me back from the brink. My body had lost the ability to get rid of waste on its own, and the buildup of toxins needed to be flushed from system—and fast.

"She's going to slip into a coma if we don't get these levels under control," I heard a doctor say. "We can't let that happen."

If I were to slip into a coma, my chances for getting a new liver would be shot. I'd be bumped off the wait list, ineligible for a new organ. With so many people waiting on lifesaving donations, there's no way they'd hold my spot. It could be a waste of a perfectly good liver. There was no way of knowing what condition I'd be in once I emerged from the coma. I could be in a vegetative state, if I woke up at all. An organ needs to be placed within hours for the transplant to be successful, and my state was just too uncertain to count on. Slipping into a coma was the big red line that couldn't be crossed. And yet, my body seemed hell bent on racing right over that very line.

I was only vaguely aware as my team set about flushing the toxins from my body. They injected a laxative into the IV fluid that was already coursing through my bloodstream. But because my body wasn't eliminating waste on its own, my team needed to find a workaround. As I slid into unconsciousness, on the brink of slipping into a comatose state, they decided to insert a rectal tube. With no time to waste, they hurried to place the tube inside me.

The searing pain dragged me back into consciousness, and a scream of agony ripped from my throat. The entire time I was in the hospital, I hadn't been allowed to take any pain medication. It would have been poison to my already besieged system. I'd suffered through countless tests without any anesthetic, but this was of another order entirely. The rectal tube was as thick as a garden hose, as unyielding as a steel pipe. I had no idea what was going on, only that the pain was unbearable. I felt violated, humiliated, and so, so angry.

I fought back against my team with everything I had.

My family could hear my furious screams from the hallway as I thrashed in my bed. I was completely out of control, lashing out in any way I could to escape the excruciating pain. When I bit the hand of my one of my nurses, I was restrained—handcuffed to my hospital bed. Later, my dad would tell me that my anguished cries sounded like something out of *The Exorcist*. It really did feel like I had been possessed, unable to communicate the alarming but very real fact that I wanted to die in order to escape the excruciating pain I was in.

Straining against the cuffs, I started to feel reality slip farther away. The fact that this moment could really exist on the continuum of my normal, happy life tested my ability to accept God's plan. Finally, having fitted tubes into every orifice of my body, my medical team retreated. I sunk back into my hospital bed, utterly drained of energy and barely able to focus as the room swirled drunkenly around me. It would take time for the toxins to leave my system, and all I could do was lie there. But as far gone as I felt, as unprecedented as this moment was, I knew that I had to find a way to accept it. As it turned out, my hard-won trust in God was stronger than I ever could have imagined.

And good thing, too—because the real tests of that trust were still to come.

***

Chapter Seven

A Helping Hand

I spent an entire day in unimaginable pain and discomfort as the toxins were flushed from my body through the rectal tube. Unable to escape the situation or communicate properly, I gave into the numbing agony. Those twenty-four hours were by far the worst of my medical crisis so far, the worst I had ever experienced in my life. But the tube proved to be a necessary evil. Little by little, the toxins were wiped from my system. Still, no one knew for certain if this effort would keep me from slipping into a coma. I was still toeing that big red line, and at any moment I could stumble right over it.

As I hovered on the brink of unconsciousness, I could feel myself detaching from my raw and aching body. Even though I knew that I was handcuffed to my hospital bed, I felt like I was looking down on the scene from somewhere else. Somewhere removed from time and space and even illness. The hospital room that I'd been confined to for more than a week faded away into a blurry haze. Blinking up into the soft light of this new space, I looked around to take stock of my surroundings.

It felt as though I was floating weightlessly, unburdened by my ravaged body, the tubes and handcuffs, the uncertainty and expectation. Casting my gaze across this new, serene landscape, I noticed a familiar silhouette far out in the distance. The everyday sounds of the hospital had become distant and dulled, as if to not distract me from what was unfolding. As I watched, the shape out ahead of me resolved into the form of a person. At once, I was struck by the sensation of intense familiarity. I recognized the man moving toward me, though it had been a while since we'd seen each other last.

Grandpa Charlie... I thought to myself, watching with wonder as the smiling face of my grandfather appeared before my eyes. *What are you doing here?*

In response, he simply smiled—that warm, familiar smile that I'd missed so terribly in the three years since he passed away. I found, remarkably, that I wasn't surprised to see him. I was too overcome with awe to be shocked or wary. My overtaxed body was, I knew, close to the end of its journey. And now here was my grandfather—coming to greet me as I drew so close to the end of my time here on Earth.

Are you here...for me? I asked him silently, drinking in the sight of this person I never thought I would see again while I lived.

In response, he simply extended his hand to me, his heavily lined palm facing upward. My heart swelled with gratitude, seeing this helping hand reaching out to me. Was he offering to hold my hand as I passed on? Lead me along that final leg of my journey? I couldn't know for sure. I could only put my faith in God and let myself be led. I reached out to my grandfather, yearning to feel his hand in mine. Whatever was in store for me, I was ready to accept it with open arms. I closed my eyes and reached with what little strength I had for my grandfather's hand. The world began to fade away, even as my fingers closed around air. My mind went blissfully blank as I gave into the moment, and put my trust in what was to come...

The excited murmuring of voices caught my ear, and I did my best to wrangle my wayward mind back to the present. It was the next day, I soon discovered. And I was still here. I blinked around, amazed by the newfound clarity of my mind. The toxins had been successfully flushed from my system, the rectal tube replaced with a less invasive bag. I'd managed not to slip into a coma, which meant that I was still eligible for a new liver.

I was genuinely surprised to find myself still alive, let alone coherent. When I saw my grandfather reach out to me, I thought for certain that he was there to lead me out of this life. I had expected to find myself on the other side, guided by my grandfather into the next phase of my journey. But instead, I was back in my room at UC. My grandfather hadn't been reaching out to lead me across the threshold of death, I realized. He had been offering me a supportive hand, a gesture of strength and encouragement. It wasn't time for me to join him. Not just yet.

With great effort, I focused my senses and took a look

around me. I was in my hospital room in the ICU as a flurry of people orbited around me. My dad and David had appeared alongside my mom and Rebecca, and the four of them listened with rapt attention as they were briefed by one of my doctors. I could tell from the amazed looks on their faces that something had shifted in our favor.

"It's an incredible stroke of luck," my doctor went on. "Now we just have to hope that a match can be found."

"And we're talking about the *national* list, right?" my dad pressed, as if scarcely able to believe what he was hearing.

"That's right, Mr. Steck," my doctor confirmed, looking over at my bed and catching my eye with a smile.

"What's going on?" I asked drowsily, looking between their hopeful faces.

"You've been bumped up," David said excitedly, a grin breaking across his face.

"Huh?" I mumbled, still trying to wrap my head around the fact that I was still here instead of with my grandfather.

"Jessica," my mom clarified. "You've been moved up from the tristate organ transplant wait-list. Right now, you're number one in the entire nation to receive a new liver."

My vision swam with surprised tears as I took in the news. The only word my baffled mind could formulate was,

How?

"Someone must be keeping an eye on you," my doctor said warmly, happy to be delivering good news to my family after such a difficult wait.

"He is," I replied softly. "Always."

When I saw my grandfather reaching out to me the day before, I thought that he had been sent by God to accompany me out of this life. As it turns out, God *did* send my grandfather to give me a helping hand that day—not out of this life, but through the trial that was my illness.

With His help, I'd made the miraculous leap to the very top of the national transplant wait list; a list with tens of thousands of names on it at any given time. After making it through a long, painful week of helpless waiting while my family and friends watched my health deteriorate, we'd finally been granted a glimmer of hope in the darkness.

"This calls for a bit of celebration, don't you think?" I heard one of my favorite nurses ask from across the room.

Still sporting all manner of tubes and wires, I raised my head to look her way. With a grateful laugh, I saw what she was holding in her hand: a lemon slushie.

Miracles really never cease, do they?

***

Chapter Eight

My Angel, Dustin

Moving up to the number one spot on the national wait list was more than just a miracle. It was a wake-up call. For the first week I'd spent in the hospital, the idea of my liver transplant had still been hypothetical. We couldn't proceed without a new organ, so I hadn't fully processed the fact that it was going to happen. Now, it was all happening so fast that I didn't even have time to be afraid of the procedure. The preparations for my transplant unfolded all around me like a surreal dance, and it was all I could do to look on in astonished wonder. I hadn't yet thought through what it would mean to receive a new liver—what getting a second shot at life would mean for someone else.

Soon after we got word that I was next in line for a new liver, my doctors had even more good news for me and my family. A new liver had become available, and it might be a match for me. I was surprised at how quickly the pieces were falling into place, and I was even more shocked to realize that I hadn't spent much time thinking about the practical realities of receiving a new liver. While this first liver turned out to be too big for my body, the false alarm gave me tremendous pause. I wasn't disappointed about not finding a match right away—I knew by then that God had the situation well under control. But for the first time, I found myself confronting the fact that in order for me to have a shot at getting my life back, someone else was going to have to lose theirs first.

Of course, the fact that I was waiting on a new liver wasn't going to bring about anyone else's death. Even if I— and the many other people waiting for organ transplants around the country—weren't in need, people would still be coming to the ends of their lives. The demand for donated organs doesn't cause anyone's death. Organ donation is a way that people can choose to give others life, even *in* death. We think about death in such black-and-white terms, as a concrete, physical reality that can't be altered. But with the miraculous science of organ transplants, death can be averted. My life had the chance to continue, despite my brush with death, because an organ transplant was possible.

But even though I understood this fact on an intellectual level, the situation still set off a barrage of emotions for me to contend with. I was excited at the prospect of having a new lease of life even as I felt terribly guilty for essentially waiting around for someone else to die. Not only that, but I couldn't help thinking about all the other names on the organ transplant list. I had leapfrogged over all of them to land in the number one spot, and I found myself feeling unworthy of this good fortune. And that was *before* my transplant became a reality.

There has never been anything sweeter, more sumptuously delicious, than a lemon slushie in the midst of an excruciating medical ordeal. The tart, icy sweetness was like ambrosia for my parched throat and chapped lips. My nurses caught on to just how much pleasure I got out of this treat, and made a habit of delivering lemon slushies right to my bed. (As if I wasn't *already* convinced that nurses are angels disguised in scrubs.)

A couple of days into my residency at the top of the national transplant wait list, a nurse named Melissa had surprised me with my favorite icy treat. As I sat in my bed, helping myself to some frozen lemony goodness, another nurse appeared in my doorway. I looked up to see the incomparable Rachel—or "Big Rachel" as she was proudly called—striding into my room.

"Well, Jessica. I've got some good news, and I've got some bad news," Rachel said, coming a stop at the foot of my bed.

"OK..." I said warily, swallowing a mouthful of slushie. "Gimme the bad first."

"The bad news," Rachel said, "is that you've got to put your slushie down."

"I knew it was too good to be true," I sighed, reluctantly handing my treat back to Melissa.

"Actually, you can't have *anything* to eat right now," Rachel went on, a huge smile spreading across her face, "because we need to start prepping you for surgery."

"Wh—what?" I exclaimed, sitting up in bed.

"That's the good news, Jessica," Rachel said. "You're getting your new liver!"

"Way to bury the lead, Rach," Melissa joked, looking as happy as I felt.

"And it's for real this time?" I pressed, still trying to wrap my head around this latest development, "It's the right size, the right blood type?"

"It's a perfect match," Rachel assured me. "You and this liver were meant to be."

June 12, 2011, after days upon days of relentless stillness and waiting, I was swept up by a sudden whirlwind of activity. As preparations continued, word spread through my friends and family that my transplant was finally going to happen. Emotions and energy were running high as I was prepped for surgery. Not only were my loved ones ecstatic about this turn of events, my medical team was thrilled on my behalf.

But even as I experiencing a wave of relief that this trial was soon to be over, I couldn't wholeheartedly celebrate the fact that a new liver had been found for me. For a transplant to be successful, an organ must be transferred from a donor to a recipient within a matter of hours. That meant whoever I was receiving this lifesaving gift from had passed away that very day. As my friends and family were thanking God for my new lease on life, there was another family somewhere out there mourning the loss of someone they loved. My new liver had just belonged to someone else—someone who was about to save my life.

And I had no idea who that person was.

"Why am I the one who gets to live?" I whispered softly, as the flurry of preparation continued all around me.

"What was that?" asked Grant, one of the nurses getting me ready to go under.

"Why do I get to be saved when my donor wasn't?" I asked, needing someone to relieve my conscience.

"That's for God to know," Grant replied simply, giving me a warm smile. "Let's just focus on getting you ready."

I nodded, blinking away tears as the anesthesia hit my bloodstream. After going so long without pain medication, the return of anesthetic to my body was nothing short of sublime. I'd been carefully bathed in preparation for surgery by my nurse Tanisha. The surgical bath, performed with hushed reverence even in the midst of this whirlwind procedure, felt like a sacred ritual. It was so soothing to feel entirely clean again. I did my best to savor these sensations of relief as I was wheeled into surgery. There was nothing more that I could do or worry about. I could relax and let things unfold as they had to.

As I slipped into unconsciousness, the last thoughts on my mind were of my anonymous donor. I felt myself drifting out of the world for a spell, into a liminal space between life and death. For the duration of my four-hour surgery, I'd have one foot in this life and one beyond it. In the last few moments before the medication took hold, I felt profoundly close to the threshold of death. So close that I could call across that final border in hopes that my donor might hear just me.

Thank you, I cried into that ultimate distance. *Thank you, whoever you are.*

It would be months before I learned even the scantest details about the person who gave me the gift of life that fateful day in June. Information about one's organ donor is not provided automatically. It's left up to the donor's family to get in touch, if that is indeed what they want. All communication is run through a third party, so that the donor's family members are in control of how much they know about the person—or people—their loved one's contributions have saved.

How much communication takes place between donors' families and organ recipients varies greatly. It all depends on the wishes of the family in question. The system is set up this way to protect families' privacy in times of unspeakable grief. Some families are eager to know the recipient of their loved one's donation, as it can be cathartic to know the person who will be safeguarding their gift. Other families prefer to have little or no communication with organ recipients. There's no right or wrong way to go about it, as each family has their own set of needs, their own way of grieving—including my donor's family.

On February 14, 2012, about eight months after my transplant, I received a letter in the mail. Given the date, I wasn't surprised by the uptick in correspondence. I got more valentines the year after my operation than perhaps ever before, from friends and family who wanted me to know just how loved I was and how happy they were to still have me in their lives. But of all the messages of love and support I received that year, there was one letter in particular that stuck with me—that will always stick with me.

It was a message from my donor's family.

The letter, delivered through a third party, was simple and direct. I held the postcard in my hands like the precious offering it was. For so long, I had wanted answers about who my donor was in life. And now, I had finally gotten my wish. As if I hadn't already received enough from this family. I took a deep, steadying breath and turned the postcard over. It read:

Organ Recipient,

I want you to know how glad I am that you now have another chance to live your life in hopes of something wonderful for you and your family. I send my prayers and best wishes to you. I am proud that Dustin's organs and tissue were able to help so many people.

Best wishes to all in hopes of a better life. My prayers

go out to you.

Sincerely,

Lewis (Dustin's dad)

And just like that, after months of wondering, I had a name for the person whose generosity had saved my life. My angel's name was Dustin. I added this fact to the small collection of things I knew about my organ donor. First, I knew that he was from Columbus, Ohio, a mere hour's drive away from my own hometown of Dayton. Second, that he was only eighteen years old when he passed away—a full ten years younger than me. And now, I knew that his name was Dustin.

I could infer a few more facts from there. I assumed that Dustin had been a boy, though I didn't know for sure. I guessed about the hallmark experiences he would have had growing up as an Ohio kid. But this small offering of information also sent a thousand other questions ricocheting around my head. What had Dustin been like in life? What were his aspirations and goals? Had he wanted to see the rest of the world as badly as I had, or was he more content to plant his flag in his home state? How had we come to share this singular connection—an eighteen-year-old boy who must have felt as invincible as I did at that age, and a twenty-eight-year-old woman who would have a second chance at life thanks to him?

But above all the questions I had about the details—how many other people had been saved by Dustin's generosity, how he had passed away, whether his family wanted to hear back from me—one overarching question continued to hang over me. Why had I survived when Dustin, a young man on the cusp of adulthood, had not?

I had been completely blindsided by my sudden illness, thinking that I was far too young to be facing death. And yet, Dustin had been a whole decade younger than me when his time on Earth came to an end. It didn't seem fair, that he should have been taken when I was spared. But of course, fairness doesn't come into the equation. Whatever happens to us in this life is what God intends to happen. But that doesn't stop us from questioning ourselves, our value to the world. We're only human, after all.

I couldn't help but wonder what I had ever done to deserve the incredible gift that Dustin had given me. I thought of myself as a good person, but how could I ever be good *enough* to live up to the privilege that is a second shot at life? I wanted to honor the generosity of Dustin and his family, to say nothing of my own family, friends, and medical team who had helped me through my trial. I knew, receiving that letter from Dustin's father, that I had a responsibility to live my life to the fullest. To take the gift of Dustin's donation and do something extraordinary with it.

But how?

***

Chapter Nine

The Eye of the Storm

After my surgery, I was drawn back into consciousness by a powerful, burning thirst. I gulped a huge breath down my parched throat as my eyes fluttered open, searching for something to focus on. As my disorientation ebbed away, I was told that my surgery had been a success. The transplant had gone off without a hitch. I was off the ventilator and only realized then how long it had been since I'd had a sip of water.

For so long, I'd been aching for something to soothe my parched throat. Thirst wasn't something I'd ever thought much about before, having always taken access to clean water for granted. But as my stay in the hospital dragged on, and I was barred from drinking any liquids, I'd stare longingly at those little papers cups as nurses delivered water to everyone but me. There was an ice machine stationed right outside my door, and I yearned for just one little chip of frozen water.

After the surgery, my wish was finally granted. I was allowed to eat ice chips again. The first time I held an ice chip on my tongue, feeling it turn to water in my mouth—that is something I'll never forget. To this day, my appreciation for water has stayed with me. Being deprived of this basic human need humbled me in a profound way. The relief and gratitude that came with that first sip of water was incredible. But even in the midst of that immense relief, I could still feel a dogged sense of apprehension tugging at my nerves. I knew, somehow, that I wasn't out of the woods just yet.

In the hours after my surgery, I felt the urgent need to speak with my father, whose relationship to prayer was strong and constant. My dad was raised in a deeply religious environment, where people didn't just pray on Sundays and when they needed help or counsel. Instead, my dad and his family embodied the idea of *living prayer*. They prayed like they drew air into their lungs, like their hearts went on beating without them having to think. To them, prayer was an active state, infusing every moment of their lives. I didn't know why, but I felt the need to stand in the light of that devotion after I woke up from my surgery.

"Dad," I murmured, reaching for him under the harsh hospital lights. "I just...I need you here with me, OK?"

"Of course," he said. "I'm not going anywhere."

I couldn't explain my sudden compulsion for closeness and protection, but that didn't stop my family from hearing my wishes. In those hours after my surgery, I felt moved to reach out to my most devout family members and friends. My aunt Barb, a woman closer to God than anyone I knew, was a great comfort when I insisted on giving her a call. Though she herself was facing a terminal cancer diagnosis, she still had such incredible reserves of strength. The fact that she used that strength to pray for me is the epitome of selflessness, in my mind.

"They're saying the surgery was successful, but I know something is wrong," I told her tearfully, my hoarse voice rasping over the phone line. "I just don't know *what...*"

"No matter what happens, remember that God is with you," Aunt Barb told me. "You're in His hands, Jessica. He won't let anything happen to you that isn't supposed to."

That was the reminder I needed most in that uncertain moment. I didn't want to hear that everything would be all right or that nothing bad was going to happen now. After all, what had my unexpected sickness taught me if not to take anything for granted, and that bad things can happen when you least expect them? What I needed to hear most after my surgery was that God was still in control, that there was nothing I could do but continue to trust him.

My mom and Rebecca were stationed in my room, as ever, discussing what would need to happen once I got out of the hospital. In all of our minds, we were through the worst of it now that the transplant had taken place. Our concerns were in the process of being dialed back from life-and-death to day-to-day.

"She's going to need our help with everything," my mom said to Rebecca. "Eating, bathing, remembering which medications to take—"

"Well, at least it's June," my sister said optimistically,

"I have my whole summer break ahead of me, so I can be there to help out."

"Thank God our family is all nurses and teachers," Mom replied. "We're gonna need all hands on deck."

My dad and David joined us in my hospital room, looking tired but relieved to have the transplant behind us. My medical team assured us that the surgery was totally successful. They urged my family to go home and get some rest while I recovered overnight. I could see that my family was reluctant to leave my side. They'd been at the hospital nearly 24/7 since I was admitted, and leaving me here alone was hard for them.

"It's OK," I assured them despite my misgivings. "You guys should really go get some sleep. I'll be fine."

"Are you sure?" Rebecca asked.

"I'm positive," I replied with as much of a smile as I could muster.

Eventually, my family was persuaded to head out. When they left for the night, I was alone with my reeling thoughts. As many times as my doctors assured me that all was well, I couldn't shake the feeling that this was just the eye of the storm. My gut told me that the rest of the tempest was still on its way.

Night settled over the hospital, and I willed myself to remember Aunt Barb's words. Nothing would happen that wasn't part of God's plan, and I had to find a way to trust that. Exercising that kind of blind trust can be a terrifying prospect in the face of total uncertainty. Letting go of the wish to control things or the idea that we even have that power is a daunting task in the best of circumstances. If I hadn't been challenged to practice radical trust in that most extreme moment of my life, I don't know if I would have ever discovered its power.

But with the encouragement of my loved ones and the power of prayer, I pushed myself to go all in. To embrace my faith in God without holding anything back. And it was this unconditional faith that carried me through everything that happened next.

***

Chapter Ten

Surrender

Early the next morning, June 13, 2011, one of my nurses arrived to check in on me. She chatted to me as she came in to do her rounds, just as usual. My nurses and I had come to enjoy an easy, friendly relationship. But that morning, I couldn't manage any light conversation.

My nurse trailed off in the middle of her sentence as my silence registered with her. My breathing had become shallow and rasping, more arduous that it should have been. As my nurse's eyes went wide, I realized that I must have looked as bad as I felt as I struggled to breathe normally.

"What? What's the matter?" I asked, my voice barely a croak.

"Your lips..." the nurse murmured, her expression hardening into stone.

"What about them?" I asked. "What's happening?"

"We need some help in here!" my nurse called out into the hallway, ignoring my questions as she switched into action mode.

"What's going on?" I rasped, glancing down at my body to see what was wrong.

My heart stopped in its tracks as I noticed the purple splotches staining my hands. They were spreading across my body, as if a bottle of ink had been overturned beneath my skin. But of course, it wasn't ink that was pooling in my body—it was blood. *Liters* of blood.

"She must have thrown a clot," the nurse said urgently, as my entire team of medical staff came rushing into the room. Usually so ready with a smile and a joke for me, they were grim and serious as they entered my room.

"Her lips are turning purple," the nurse relayed to the rest of the team. "We don't have any time to waste."

The steady, metronomic beeps of the machines monitoring my vital signs began to throw off their consistent rhythm. When that reliable sound began to falter, I knew that something was seriously wrong. The feeling of dread that had been tugging at my heart since I woke up from my surgery finally made sense. My body and spirit must have known that the ordeal wasn't over just yet.

"Her blood pressure is dropping," one of my nurses said, as she and the team sprung into action all around me.

"My family…" I muttered. "Someone has to call them…"

"Don't worry about that right now," one of the nurses told me. "We'll take care of it."

My parents were staying in a hotel just over the state line in Kentucky. They were out on an early morning Target run, picking up some travel essentials, when I threw the blot clot. They got the call that I was heading back into surgery while standing in the an aisle of the superstore. Without a second thought, they dropped what they were doing and rushed back to my side, calling my siblings en route.

Back at the hospital, my medical team was moving like a well-oiled machine, maneuvering around my bed with single-minded intensity. I watched as if from very far away, as the pain that I'd grown accustomed to through all of this process began to swell and grow. It coursed through my body, stunning me with its sudden breadth and vigor. And the pain was only just getting started.

I couldn't focus on my doctor's words as he tried to explain what was happening to me or the beautifully calibrated movements of my nurses. Everything was blotted out by the searing pain. The struggle to keep breathing was incredible. I could barely even sense my body moving through space as I was rushed into surgery once again. I thought I had learned, in the lead-up to my transplant, what excruciating pain felt like.

I was wrong.

A blood clot had formed somewhere in my body, setting off a cascade of internal damage. My abdomen became flooded with blood, about twelve liters in all. My blood pressure had plummeted to the point of being essentially nonexistent. But most alarmingly of all, my new liver had detached inside my body. After all that time spent waiting and praying, all of our elation at the arrival of my donor's gift, my body had refused to accept this saving grace without a fight. Dustin's liver was going to go to waste, and I felt personally responsible for that tragedy. As I was wheeled back into surgery, I was certain that this was finally it.

This was how I was going to die.

My failing body was laid out on the operating table. A huge, surgical spotlight flared to life overhead, bathing me in its sharp, unsparing blaze. Above me, doctors and nurses rushed around in a state of sustained, controlled chaos. A heavy hush had fallen over the room like a thick blanket. For all the frenzied, frenetic movement going on above me, the operating room was deathly silent. It was as though my doctors and nurses were already standing vigil over my body. It truly felt like I was already gone.

I was in such incredible pain, drowning in the fluid that was filling my lungs, that I tried to dissociate from my physical form. It was like I was already preparing to say goodbye to the body that had carried me through my twenty-eight years of life. This body had been good to me, even as I criticized and complained about it. Even as I toiled to make it smaller, fitter, and more attractive, never giving it the full acceptance and love it deserved, it had never faltered—not until now.

I made a promise, right then and there, that if I made it out of this alive, I would learn to love the body God had given me. If I had been able to accept myself as I was in the first place, I wouldn't be in this life-threatening situation now. It wasn't drugs or alcohol that had put my body in peril—it was my misguided ideas about beauty and perfection. I knew that if I lived through this, I'd have to find a way to throw off the shackles of unattainable beauty standards and societal pressure. I'd have to embrace my body with all my might, to make finally amends with myself as I was meant to be. I just hoped I'd get a chance to make things right.

As the pain reached a numbing, unimaginable fever pitch, I felt certain that I had reached the point of no return. I needed to get ready to say goodbye. I was so exhausted, so worn out from fighting for my life. I wanted to be free of this suffering—and just as urgently, I wanted to set my loyal, unfailing friends and family free. They'd been through enough already, seeing me through this crisis without a second thought. They deserved to rest, and so did I.

The doctors did their best to control my worsening condition. They secured a ventilator around my mouth and nose—a device that might as well be classified as an instrument of torture, as far as I'm concerned. I gagged on the ventilator ceaselessly, choking on the intrusive tubes even as I was being suffocated by the fluid in my lungs. Even my teeth were aching as the ventilator worked to keep me alive. All I could do was try to extricate my mind from my body to escape the pain.

I watched the scene unfold from outside my own body.

Closing my eyes, I started to let my mind go peacefully blank. I pulled my focus away from the ventilator, the pain, the chaotic activity churning all around me. As I willed my spirit to rise above the fray, to move beyond the body that had been my home in life.

In my mind's eye, an imagined scene began to unfold. I pictured myself lying entirely naked beneath the glow of the surgical spotlight. I was curled up in the fetal position, white as a sheet. My doctors lay my lifeless body down on a cold metal tray—the kind that holds scalpels and other medical instruments. From beyond my own body, I said goodbye to myself. The spotlight hanging over me gave way to a new light. *The* light. And I moved toward it, unafraid. I was ready to die.

As I lay there choking on my ventilator, I didn't feel defeated or cowardly for being prepared to die. I *wanted* to die. I didn't want to feel this pain any longer. This was no kind of life. As I finally gave myself over to what was happening, I regained the peace of mind I'd fought so hard to discover in the lead-up to my transplant. I knew that this was the moment I had been waiting for, the moment that would be the ultimate test of my faith. I had to be brave enough to put myself entirely in God's hands.

I gave myself over to this new state, picturing God waiting there for me. Placing myself in his care, I could feel his love wrapping me up in strong, protective arms. The relief that came as I let myself be cradled in God's arms like

I was one of his lambs was a real, physical sensation. I knew that I could stay here as long as I needed—for an eternity, if that's what He had in mind. I was ready to accept whatever was to become of me, even if that meant that this was end of my time on Earth.

Finally, at long last, I had found the strength to surrender.

Surrender isn't an act that is usually looked upon kindly. Mostly, it's used in reference to a person who is giving in to an enemy, submitting to an unkind, hostile authority for lack of character or determination. In our hyperaggressive, competitive world, we're taught from an early age that surrender is for cowards and weaklings. Surrender is meant to be a shameful act, something to be avoided at all costs. But in my experience, surrender is something to embrace with open arms.

I lingered in that place of peace and protection throughout the worst stretch of my second surgery. It was so amazing to have finally arrived in a state of surrender after spending so much of my life needing to be in control that I didn't want to leave right away. And in truth, I almost didn't. I learned later that I had died on the operating table as my doctors worked to control the damage caused by the blood clot. I really had left my body and gone to God in that moment. He revealed Himself to me when I needed Him most, and that wasn't His only appearance, either.

After my second surgery, I was sewn up once again, my

liver successfully reattached. I was transferred back to my room, still hooked up to the ventilator. The pressure on my lungs was unbearable—I still felt like I was drowning inside my own body. Barely conscious through the searing agony, I reached for my mother. She was there at my bedside as ever as I begged for a whiteboard, desperate to communicate something to her but unable to speak around the tangle of tubes that had been shoved down my mouth and nose. She obliged, holding the board steady as I clenched a marker in my weak grasp. I could only manage to write a single word, but it communicated everything I wanted to say:

Surrender.

My mom saw the word scrawled out on the white board and the desperation in my eyes.   "Can we sit her up?" she asked the nurses. "It might help with the pain."

My nurse, Mike, helped me sit up in my hospital bed. I drew a breath, amazed at how this small shift took the pressure off my lungs. The drowning sensation that had been plaguing me since I threw the blood clot was finally relieved. I felt a wave of euphoria wash over me as the world came back into focus around me. Someone was playing the local gospel station on the radio, and my foot began to tap gently in time to the music. Light from the window of my hospital room glowed against my cheek, and I turned to look at the world outside.

As I gazed out the window, something caught my eye.

Or rather, someone. I saw a man standing there, backlit by the bright sun. He was intensely familiar to me. How many times had I seen his image in the course of my life? The long hair, the flowing white robe, the open and accepting eyes... It was Jesus Christ Himself I saw through the window, flanked on either side by a young lamb. He stood over them as He gazed up at me. And I knew in that moment that He'd been keeping watch over me, too.

"Is that better?" my nurse asked, bringing me back to the moment at hand.

I swung my gaze back to the hospital room, amazed by what I had just seen.

"Yes...thank you," I whispered, on the verge of tears.

"Of course," Mike smiled. "We're glad to have you back, Jessica."

I smiled back, my heart bursting with joy and gratitude. It truly did feel as though I had come back to Earth from some other place entirely. I looked around my hospital room with new eyes. I could see how lucky I was to still be alive, even as I could see just how much work it would take to fully recover. It was as though I had been reborn, and, like any newborn, I had a lot to learn.

***

Chapter Eleven

The First Steps Toward Recovery

One of the first things I tackled was walking again. For someone who used to spend hours of every week dancing, all this stillness felt very strange. But wouldn't you know it, it was music that awakened that dancer's spirit in me again and brought me to my feet. That local gospel music channel I'd heard just after my surgery became a mainstay in my recovery. Once I was sitting up again, my foot kept tapping to that music, as if I was getting ready to leap into a dance routine. The music motivated me as I took my first steps postsurgery and kept me going even when that going got particularly tough.

My body was still incredibly swollen and bruised from retaining so much fluid. Usually, my weight hovered around 130 pounds, but by then it had risen to 188. I almost had to laugh at my concerns all those months ago, when my ankles first began to subtly swell. What would I have thought if I could see myself now? Maybe I would have been panicked by my physical transformation before. But there in the hospital, I was far too busy being grateful for my new lease on life to be concerned about something as minor as weight gain.

Everything was new again now that I had literally come back to life. The unimaginable pleasure that came with taking my first sip of water absolutely blew my mind. This tiny, everyday act that I'd completely taken for granted before was nothing short of euphoric now. I tried to memorize the feeling of each new sensation—my first sip of water, my first bite of food, the indescribable majesty that was a Happy Meal from McDonald's someone brought me in the recovery ward. The first time I was able to use the bathroom on my own was so freeing—not just because my body was functioning again, but because it meant I wouldn't have to rely on the care of others for the rest of my life. I wanted to remember just how grateful I was for all these small miracles because every time I glanced down at my new scar, I was reminded that someone had died so that I could experience all of these things again.

The incision made in my abdomen was shaped like an upside-down *Y*, almost like the spokes of a peace sign. It certainly didn't invoke the word *peace* at first. Immediately postop, the site of my transplant was run through with metallic staples, holding my midsection together. But as the incision began to heal, I found that I wasn't at all perturbed by my new scar. It was a constant reminder of the gift I had received from my angel, Dustin, a reminder to be grateful and to live in the moment. Even now, many years later, when I find myself getting caught up in the minutiae of daily life, the insignificant annoyances and frustrations, one glance at my scar is all it takes to recenter my perspective and restore my sense of gratitude.

You never think that something like this is going to happen to you. But my scar is a reminder that it *did* happen and that something else unexpected could always be waiting around the bend. I don't say this out of a sense of fatalism or paranoia, but because it's the truth. We can't know ahead of time what God has in store for us. We can only do our best to love the people in our lives, live up to our full potential, and always, always be grateful for what we have.

My condition finally started to improve with the invaluable help of my friends, family, and medical team. They all provided constant motivation and support as I began the process of healing. The only member of my family who couldn't be with me then was ChaCha, who wasn't allowed in the hospital. But even she did her part from afar, inspiring me to work hard on my recovery so I could get home to her as soon as possible.

I needed a lot of assistance during those last few days in the hospital as I prepared to head home. Bathing, eating, and even brushing my teeth were too much for me to tackle on my own. At twenty-eight, it was strange to have my mother caring for me as if I were a newborn again. I had to learn to check my ego and pride and accept help, even with the most basic tasks. I had to accept that getting myself back into good health was going to be a team effort. Luckily, I happened to have the best team a girl could ever ask for.

As I was moved from my room in the ICU up to the recovery ward, it finally began to sink in that I was going to make it. I was really going home. This reversal was hard to wrap my head around at first. I had been so prepared to die. But now, I was going to be released. What would my life look like on the other side of this experience? I was going to step back into my life as a busy, young professional—only, with an entirely new outlook on life. A life that I owed to someone else.

It was difficult to come to terms with the guilt I felt, even in midst of my gratitude and wonder. There was no getting around the fact that I was alive because an eighteen-year-old boy from Ohio had died. I knew on some level that the truth was more complicated than that, of course. Dustin wouldn't have lived if I had happened to die. I couldn't have offered up my life in exchange for his. But I needed time to mourn for this person I had never met, this person who I now carried in my body and my heart. I'd never met my organ donor, but now our lives were inextricably linked. I had to go on living as best I could—not just for my sake, but for Dustin's as well. I would be living for both of us now.

I sat on my neatly made bed on the recovery floor, looking around my room for the last time. It was June 20, twenty-one days after I had first been admitted to UC. In three short weeks, my life had been completely transformed. And now, at long last, I was being released. I was finally going home.

"You gonna miss us?" one of my nurses asked with a smile, checking in on me one last time before I headed out.

"Like crazy," I told her. "I don't know what I would have done without you guys."

"Someone had to keep the lemon slushies coming for you!" she laughed. "Just remember, pay it forward."

"Of course," I nodded. "I promise, I will."

My dad poked his head into my room as the nurse moved onto another patient. He had come to pick me up from the hospital while my mom got everything ready for me at home. I'd be staying with them for a few weeks, as I'd still need a lot of help as I got my strength back. I was so fortunate that my mom was a nurse. I can't imagine how hard this would have been without her knowledgeable oversight, not to mention my dad's patience and my siblings' generous support. I simply couldn't imagine going through something like this without a family like mine.

"Ready to hit the road?" Dad asked, grabbing my bag of belongings that sat on the bed beside me.

"Yep. Let's do it," I replied, accepting his hand as he helped me up.

We made our way out of the hospital together, taking our time so that I could keep up. As we went, my nurses and doctors said their farewells, wishing me luck and a speedy recovery. I'd only met these people a few weeks ago, but they had already come to feel like family. I swore to myself that I'd do my best to make them proud as I ventured back out into the world.

"Here we go," Dad said as we stepped up to the front doors of UC.

I squeezed his hand a little tighter, taking a deep breath to steady myself. Dad pushed open the heavy front doors, and I took a small step over the threshold. After three weeks of being confined a hospital bed, my first breath of fresh air brought tears to my eyes. As we made our way to Dad's car, I looked all around me, thinking that I'd never seen anything so beautiful—and this was while we were still in the *parking lot*.

Dad helped me into the passenger seat of his car, lending me some of the strength he'd built up over years of hard, physical work. I would come to depend on that strength so much in the weeks I spent recovering at home. After making sure I was buckled in, Dad walked around to the driver's side and started up his old, reliable car. It was time to go home.

My nose was practically pressed up against the window as we made our way back to Dayton. I'd been along the route from my hometown to Cincinnati more times than I could count—but that day, I was utterly transfixed along the way. It was surreal, encountering all of these familiar sights with my new perspective, all these things I never thought I'd see again. Simply getting to ride in a car felt like a luxury, and it took a while for me to believe that it was really happening.

That sense of wonder persisted as we arrived at my

parents' house, where my mom and siblings were waiting for me. I let myself be led inside in a daze. My mom had the place all set up for me. I would stay here and receive twenty-four-hour care, thanks to her and my dad. I was so overwhelmed by the lengths to which my family had gone to care for me. It was thanks to them that I had the mental and spiritual strength to make it through my stay at the hospital. And now, they were going to see me through my recovery, too.

But my family wasn't quite done surprising me that day.

My ears perked up as I heard a familiar rumbling sound from the front of my parents' house. It was the growl of an old truck engine advancing up along the driveway. A tight knot rose in my throat as I glanced out the front window, confirming what I already knew in my heart. There in the driveway was Grandpa Marion's silver Chevy pickup. I'd know the sound of that truck anywhere.

"Look's like someone's here to see you," my mom said, her voice thick with emotion.

I waddled slowly out onto the porch, still getting used to the feeling of the ground beneath my feet. As I stepped outside, Grandpa Marion eased himself down from the pickup. He lowered his oxygen tank onto the ground beside him and raised his eyes to mine. We took each other in—him with his oxygen tank, me with my bruised and swollen body—and shared a smile of camaraderie.

We didn't speak a word as I made my way slowly across the yard to greet him. He didn't get around too well by then, and I wasn't about to make my grandpa overdo it, even in my compromised state. He had one arm slung over the bed of his pickup truck, supporting himself as he waited to greet me. I followed suit, steadying myself against the reliable old pickup as I reached my grandpa. He's never been a man of many words, but the look he gave me as I stood before him that day spoke volumes.

"You made it," he said, his eyes welling up.

A single tear rolled down his cheek as he looked me over—the first tear I'd ever seen him shed.

"Are you OK, Grandpa?" I asked, reaching for his hand.

"I'm just... I'm so happy you're home," he said gruffly, giving my hand a squeeze.

It struck me as we stood there together that he was wearing his same old uniform of jeans and a white T-shirt. The same outfit I had asked to buried in just a couple of weeks ago. It's amazing how much can happen to a person in such a short time. As it turned out, I didn't need to pick out what I wanted to wear in my casket just yet. But my time at UC had reframed my entire outlook on life. From that day on, I knew that there was no time to waste. I'd been given a second chance, and I intended to make the most of it.

***

Chapter Twelve

Gathering My Strength

The next six weeks of my life were dedicated to getting back on my feet. Though my medical team at UC had done a fantastic job of fixing me up, there was still a lot of healing that needed to happen. Not only did my body need some more time to adjust, my mind and spirit did as well. There was a lot that I still needed to process about my experience in the hospital, the reality of my liver transplant, and how my life would be different moving forward.

In short, I needed to have a good, long think.

Getting well required energy, patience, and a whole slew of pharmaceuticals. For a while there, I was taking more than forty pills a day in addition to insulin shots and finger pricks to monitor my blood sugar. My mom oversaw my medication, since she knew the most about what each pill did and how often it needed to be taken. I have no idea how someone without her medical expertise could keep that much information straight—especially if they were still swimming through a postsurgery fog. But luckily, my mom was clear-headed as ever and kept me on track.

You can't expect to take forty pills a day without experiencing some major side effects. The medications I was taking led to relentless insomnia, bouts of shaking, bone and muscle pain, headaches, loss of appetite, and even hallucinations. It was important to steer clear of anything that might carry germs that could lead to an infection, including something as small as the foil of a restaurant butter packet.

Though I was grateful to be home recovering, I dealt with my fair share of anxiety during the first weeks of my recovery. I was constantly paranoid about germs and infection. After what happened when I threw the blood clot, I was still convinced that something would go wrong. I even had visions of my new liver falling out of my body. My mind was playing tricks on me—and they were very convincing tricks.

Not only did I have to contend with vivid hallucinations and crippling anxiety, but I also had to find a way to come to terms with the immense guilt I was feeling. It still pained me to know that I was alive because Dustin had lost his life. I wished there was a way I could thank him and his family, even though I knew it was important to respect their privacy. I didn't know how to grieve for someone I'd never met, and couldn't quite explain my guilt to others. Eventually, I'd learn to live with this feeling, but in those first few weeks, it was incredibly hard to understand my warring emotions.

Though it would take me quite a while longer to come to terms with my feelings of guilt and gratitude, some other aspects of recovery were easier to tackle. With my family's help, I worked through and around my side effects and kept pressing on. Everyone did their part to help me fully recover, even ChaCha. From the moment I arrived home from the hospital, she never left my side. She slept beside me, calmly kept me company as I rested, and offered me all the love she had to offer. She may have been a tiny dog, but her heart was enormous.

Slowly but surely, my strength returned. In a matter of weeks, I was back to working out with light weights, rebuilding the muscle mass I had lost in the hospital. I wanted to get back out into the world of the living as quickly as possible. For someone who was used to working hard and putting herself out there, being benched for three weeks was totally crazy-making. I needed to jump back into the game. I couldn't be contained. I was *ready*.

By the time six weeks had passed, the peace sign incision on my abdomen had healed into a scar. The staples had been removed, and I'd been diligently applying ointment to make sure it didn't get infected. Every time I stood before my mirror tending to my scar, I couldn't help but think about what a younger version of myself would have to say about the sudden appearance of this mark. I'd obsessed over my stomach for so many years, after all. The Jessica of yesteryear might very well have been horrified by the scars marring my abs. But now, looking at my scar only reminded me how lucky I was to have made it through my sickness. I no longer cared about whether or not my body was perfect. I was ready to embrace it, scars and all. My scars weren't evidence of violence, but the lifesaving power of love and generosity.

Who wouldn't want to be reminded of that once in a while?

In the long weeks of my recovery, I realized it wasn't just my physical scar that I would be left with after this experience. I'd been scarred mentally and emotionally, too. That's not to say that I felt wronged by the experience of my liver transplant. On the contrary, I was absolutely floored by the kindness, generosity, and faith that was showered upon me throughout the ordeal. But living through the extreme pain that went along with my sickness and the complications that occurred in the hospital was something I would never forget. That feeling of complete vulnerability and impenetrable uncertainty had left its mark on my spirit. But just as with my physical scar, I wasn't ashamed of my mental scarring at all. I knew that having experienced these things would make me a stronger, more empathetic person, and inspire me to be even more driven than I had been before.

All of my scars—be they physical, mental, or emotional—are constant reminders of what I've been through. To this day, they remind me of the precious gift I was given by a complete stranger: the gift of life. They remind me to take nothing for granted, to pray for those in need, and to be there for the people I love. I'm thankful for my scars, not ashamed of them. Without them, not only would I not be here, I would never have grown into the person I am today.

And that would be a shame, because I'm awfully fond of the person I've become.

Some people were surprised when I decided to go back to work six weeks after being released from the hospital. Honestly, though, I'm not sure I could have sat at home any longer. My experience had ignited a new sense of drive and purpose inside of me, and I was chomping at the bit to dive back into life. Thanks to the excellent care my family had given me, I was soon well enough to return to my sales job. I picked up where I left off the day I had to call out of work for my liver transplant. I was ready and raring to go.

I'd chosen to work in sales because I knew it was a job that could take me anywhere in the world I wanted to go. My company had offices all over the United States, and by the time I was back at work, I knew that I wanted to make a change. All my life, I'd dreamed of living in a big, bustling city. Somewhere I could make a fresh start and embrace as my chosen home. In my mind, there was no bigger or better city out there than New York—so that's exactly where I set my sights on landing.

Having always been good at networking, I channeled all my post-transplant energy into making new connections within my company. I went above and beyond the call of duty, driving myself to be the best employee I could be. But even as I worked hard, I brought a new sense of balance to my life. I knew that I couldn't let myself burn out again, that I had to care for and love my body in an entirely new way. But instead of being slowed down by my new understanding of self-care, I found that I was able to work even harder when I was taking care of myself properly.

Who would have thought?

I was determined to prove to my bosses that I was ready for a promotion. It didn't take them long to notice my renewed commitment and bolstered attitude. Pretransplant, I was battling against fatigue and other mysterious symptoms that distracted me from my job. But now, I was totally focused. Before the year was out, my bosses made me the offer of a lifetime. I was given the opportunity to relocate to New York City for a promotion. I'd never lived outside of Ohio in my life, but I accepted the offer in a heartbeat.

I had no idea what living in New York would be like, or whether my small-town self would fit in there. But something was drawing me to New York City, something that felt bigger than me. My intuition was telling me this was the right way forward, the way that God had planned for me. And so, I made the decision to brave the Big Apple.

And it would turn out to be the best choice I ever made.

"New York?" my mom exclaimed when I told my parents and siblings the news about my promotion and impending move.

"That's right," I said, an excited smile spreading across my face. "My bosses made me a great offer. It's going to be a huge step up in my career."

"But...you can't go all the way to *New York*," my mom insisted, looking around at the rest of my family, hoping someone would back her up.

"Why not?" Rebecca asked. "Jess will be a natural there."

"I think it's awesome news," David put in.

"Proud of you, honey," Dad said, smiling at me from across the room.

My mom, however, was not convinced. Not at all. She and my dad had both been born and raised in Ohio. They had married young and started their own family, always staying close to home. My mom had moved out of the city to marry my dad. She didn't know anyone but her new husband when she first moved out—until I was born, that is. My mom had always been incredibly invested in her kids and never wanted us to stray very far. I'm sure she never expected one of us to pick up and move to New York, of all places, but I couldn't deny myself this dream. And I knew she wouldn't want me to either, in the end.

"You guys helped me become strong enough to make this change," I told my family, with my eyes on my mom. "And now, I'm ready to tackle the next chapter of my life. I've always wanted to live in a big city, and New York...it just feels right. I can't explain it, but I need you to trust me on this. I need you to support me."

My mom met my steady gaze, and for the first time since my transplant, I caught a glimmer of sadness in her eyes.

"But who's going to take care of you out there?" she asked.

I was struck by her question. What mother hasn't wondered the exact same thing at some point as her children grow up? Of course, not every mother has brought her eldest daughter back from the brink of death by liver failure, but still. The universal nature of her concern nearly moved me to tears.

"I can take care of myself, Mom," I said gently, as the rest of my family looked on. "And I owe that to you guys."

It would still take a while for my mom to come around to the idea of my move, but by then, it was already in the works. Eleven months after I nearly died, I was ready to take on the biggest adventure of my life. I was ready to make my family, friends, colleagues, and medical team proud.

What was this second chance at life for, if not that?

***

Chapter Thirteen

The Adventure of a Lifetime

I fell for New York City the second I arrived. For a small-town girl from Ohio, I learned the ropes pretty quickly. The noise and commotion were intimidating at first, to be sure, but I was up for the challenge. This was exactly the kind of energy I had craved my whole life. I'd always dreamed of being one of the striving trailblazers that made New York City great. And at long last, I could count myself among their number.

Moving to New York was an admittedly insane thing to do so soon after major surgery. The pace of New York City life is breakneck on a slow day. I went from driving everywhere to pounding the pavement on the daily. I'd get winded climbing endless sets of subway stairs and trudging the several long blocks to the grocery store, but I was determined to get used to it. After growing up in single-family houses, moving into a tiny apartment was a crazy bit of culture shock. I couldn't help but laugh as I made my way through the gritty, germ-ridden city, thinking back to my recovery, when I wasn't even allowed to handle a packet of butter. Things sure do change fast when you're living your life to the fullest.

My transition into New York living wasn't without its difficult moments. I certainly didn't go from zero to *Sex in the City* overnight. A strange paradox about living in a big city is that you can end up feeling incredibly lonely, even when you're surrounded by people. And seeing as I was living away from my family and close-knit group of friends for the first time in my life after an incredibly intense experience, there were some pretty lonesome nights to contend with at first.

Luckily, the smallest member of my Ohio family had made the move to New York with me. ChaCha was there to help me through my transition to New York life, just like she'd been there throughout my recovery. We explored the city together, taking long walks to get accustomed to our new surroundings. ChaCha was fearless facing those bustling streets (not to mention a couple Chihuahua-sized subway rats). Our big move solidified our already close bond. I'll always be grateful to her for being by my side as I began my New York story.

I celebrated the first anniversary of my liver transplant shortly after arriving in New York. It was hard to believe just how far I'd come in those twelve months. I'd buckled down and saved enough money to pay off my medical bills, and I was ready to embrace my newfound sense of freedom. Making it through the ordeal that was my transplant had inspired me to be more spontaneous. And now that I was in the Big Apple, there were infinite opportunities to try new things. From music and museums to restaurants and boutiques, I was drinking in everything the city had to offer. But I couldn't have known when I first arrived just how much I would gain from my new home.

One weekend after I had been living in New York for a few months, some new friends invited me to come down to the Jersey shore with them. I accepted happily, eager to blow off some steam from my new job. I'd found my way back into a fitness routine that made me feel great in my body, and was excited to hit the beach. I was no longer working out to punish myself, but to celebrate everything my body could do in its new healthy state. I'd never felt so comfortable in my own skin before. I thought I had just opted into a weekend away, but the trip turned out to be much more momentous than that.

My friends and I were at a party down the shore one night, laughing and dancing the night away. I made no attempt to disguise my abdominal scars, even in my midriff-baring beach wear. People always surprised me with how positive and encouraging they were when they heard about my experience. I had been somewhat worried that people would jump to conclusions or judgments when they learned about my transplant, but instead they tended to show compassion and curiosity above all.

I was having a blast, feeling relaxed and happy to be partying at the beach. I only knew a few people at the party, but I was excited to be making some new acquaintances. I'm a people person at heart, and my years in sales have taught me how to strike up a conversation with just about anyone.

I was out on the back patio of the venue, catching some of the cool, salty breeze off the ocean, when a man walked up to me and introduced himself.

His name was Michael, and I was taken in by his friendly smile and open attitude right away. Before either of us knew it, we'd been talking for most of the night. We got along so well and found so much common ground that the hours had just flown by. I learned that he lived and worked in New Jersey, right off the George Washington Bridge. We made plans to meet up in New York sometime in the future. When we parted ways that night, I hoped that I would see him again. I wasn't dead set on being in a relationship at that point in my life, but I knew I definitely wanted to get to know Michael better.

As we spent time together back in the city, I eventually opened up about my transplant. I didn't feel the need to hide this experience from anyone, but I also didn't go out of my way to lead with it. Believe it or not, dropping "Hey, I died on the operating table for a sec!" into casual conversation can be kind of a mood killer. But even as I shared some of the more harrowing aspects of my experience with Michael, he never flinched or shied away from the subject. My liver transplant was part of my story, after all. And soon, it became clear that Michael was going to be part of my story, too.

Michael didn't just offer a patient, sympathetic ear when it came to my past. He empathized deeply with my struggles, having learned through his own experiences just how fleeting life can be. Michael lost his brother on 9/11, a tragedy that hit the New Jersey community they grew up in especially hard. His family set up a scholarship in his brother's name at a high school in New Jersey to benefit their hometown and honor his memory. When Michael and I met, his father was battling cancer. Hurricane Sandy had hit New York and New Jersey right before we ran into each other at that party, reminding us both just how quickly devastation can strike. It was our shared understanding of just how short life can be that laid the groundwork for our relationship.

Our experiences of loss had inspired us both to live at full volume, to make time for what was important. And before long, Michael was one of the most important parts of my life. Our relationship deepened as the months went on, with each of us encouraging and supporting the other in matters of career and life alike. By the time the second anniversary of my transplant came around, I was falling for Michael—and I was falling *hard*. The day of that important anniversary, Michael met me at the ferry from Manhattan, as he often did. But instead of his usual Dr. Michael Zampieri dentist's lab coat, he was in slacks and a button-down carrying flowers.

My heart swelled as I took in the sight of him, dressed up for my special occasion. The fact that he understood how important this day was to me spoke volumes about his character. I stepped down off the ferry to meet him, this man who had so swiftly became a major part of my life. Though he didn't propose that night, I still think of it as the moment I knew that I wanted to spend my life with him. Once again, I had to thank God for giving me the courage to come to New York, where I not only thrived in my career, but thrived in love as well.

Michael and I were married in 2016, celebrating with our loved ones in my hometown of Dayton, Ohio. There was so much to be thankful for that day—the fact that Michael and I had found each other in the big city, our health and happiness, the love of our family and friends. But as I stepped into this next phase of my life with Michael by my side, I made sure to pause and thank the person whose gift had made that beautiful day possible—my angel, Dustin.

God had brought Dustin and I together in a singular sort of union that June day five years earlier, just as he brought Michael and I together in marriage. Without Dustin's gift, this wonderful new phase of my life wouldn't have had the chance to unfold. This entire chapter of my story—moving to New York, meeting the love of my life, finding success in my career—would never have been written without my organ donor. And that is something that I will never, ever take for granted.

These days, Michael and I still live just outside of New York City. I can't imagine a better place to set down roots. As a dentist, Michael works hard to improve his patients' lives, but he makes plenty of time for the things that matter outside of work, too. He and I go out of our way to spend as much as possible together, enjoying each others' company and experiencing new things. We're both so happy to have found each other in such a huge city, and we mean to make the most of our life together. After weathering our fair share of hardship and loss, Michael and I have every intention of putting as much love and hope back into the world as possible. It's the least we can do.

You can never know how a single person will change the course of your destiny, how the generosity of a perfect stranger can be the difference between life and death. I certainly don't claim to have all the answers to Life's Big Questions, but I do think my liver transplant taught me a thing or two all the same. I discovered the healing power of love and prayer, an abiding, awestruck appreciation for my friends and family, and the transformative potential in surrendering to God's plan. I saw firsthand just how much we are capable of giving to others. And I learned how important it is that we all give back, whatever and however we can.

***

Epilogue

Since my transplant experience at the University of Cincinnati Medical Center, I have become a committed advocate for organ donation. I've spoken of my own lifesaving transplant and worked with many advocacy groups to spread the word about this vital service. Every year, thousands of Americans' lives are saved and improved thanks to the precious gifts of organ donors. That's thousands of stories as true and harrowing as mine, thousands of people who are alive and well and making their lasting mark on the world thanks to organ donation.

I've worked with some truly incredible organizations and inspiring individuals in my work as an advocate and activist. It's my goal to educate others about organ donation and to bring awareness to this vital system. There is so much essential research being done on the subject of organ transplants, and I want to do what I can to amplify those important efforts. I've lent my voice and story to organizations like the Columbia Transplant Forum and Donate Life. I believe that it's important for people to hear from those of us who have personal experience with the miracle of organ donation. I want to empower people to become organ donors themselves and educate them about how much good they can do by choosing to do so.

But getting more people to sign up as organ donors

isn't the only goal of my activism. I also want to reach out to young women who are dealing with the same struggles I've encountered in my life. Young women face an incredible amount of pressure to be perfect, and the pursuit of that unattainable standard can be a detriment to their health and happiness. I want girls and young women to learn what it took me many years and a life-threatening medical crisis to understand—that they are so much more than their looks alone.

All of my advocacy efforts are a tribute to my donor, Dustin. I would not be here today if Dustin had not opted to become an organ donor. At the age of eighteen, he made a decision that had the power to save multiple lives. Just imagine what would be possible if more of us decided to embrace that power. For myself, I know that I would love nothing more than to pay Dustin's gift forward, should something happen to me down the line. After being granted this incredible second chance at life, being able to give someone the same gift would, in my eyes, be the perfect end to my story.

***

If you're interested in learning more about organ donation, you can find more information through these organizations:

http://lifepassiton.org/

http://www.donatelifeohio.org/

https://www.donatelife.net/

https://www.njsharingnetwork.org/

http://www.liveonny.org/

https://organize.org/

http://www.transplantforum.org/

You can also learn about how to become an organ donor in your state through the Department of Health and Human Services:

https://organdonor.gov/register.html

Thank you

To my family and friends who have supported and prayed for me then and now:

My husband, Michael Zampieri

My parents, Susan and Tom Steck

My sister, Rebecca Steck

My brother and sister-n-law, David and Hayley Steck

My in-laws, Robert (deceased)and Patricia Zampieri

My brother-n-law and sister-n-law, Stuart and Jeannie Schlesinger

My Grandparents, Marion (deceased) and Alberta Steck, Charlie (deceased) and Julie Petrof

Aunts, Uncles and Cousins

Friends

The University of Cincinnati Health Hospital doctors and nurses

Life Connection of Ohio

Donate Life Ohio

Columbia University Medical Center

The Transplant Forum